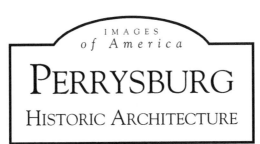

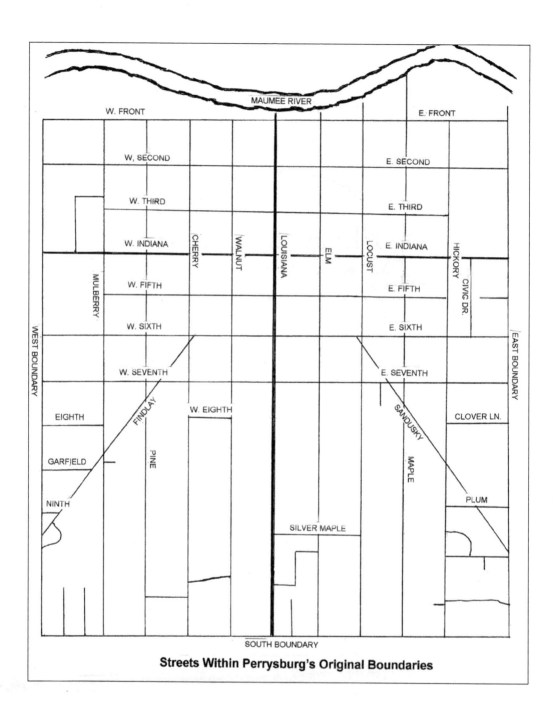

Streets Within Perrysburg's Original Boundaries

IMAGES of America

PERRYSBURG
HISTORIC ARCHITECTURE

C. Robert Boyd

ARCADIA
PUBLISHING

Copyright © 2005 by C. Robert Boyd
ISBN 978-1-5316-1950-3

Published by Arcadia Publishing
Charleston, South Carolina

Library of Congress Catalog Card Number: 2005928472

For all general information contact Arcadia Publishing at:
Telephone 843-853-2070
Fax 843-853-0044
E-mail sales@arcadiapublishing.com
For customer service and orders:
Toll-Free 1-888-313-2665

Visit us on the Internet at www.arcadiapublishing.com

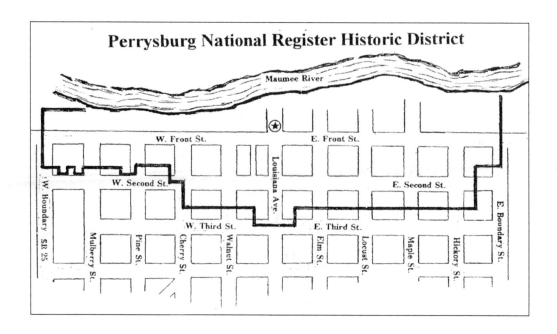

Contents

Acknowledgments		6
Introduction		7
1.	1820–1830	9
2.	1830–1840	15
3.	1840–1850	23
4.	1850–1860	39
5.	1860–1870	49
6.	1870–1880	61
7.	1880–1890	77
8.	1890–1900	85
9.	1900–1910	93
10.	1910–1930	103
Architectural Features		126
Index		127

ACKNOWLEDGMENTS

An author gets his name printed prominently in his book, but many people who make it possible are not so acknowledged. Therefore, I offer with my thanks the names of the good people to whom I am indebted: Dr. John Ahern, who proposed Arcadia Publishing's Images of America series as a way to combine and preserve previously researched descriptions of Perrysburg's buildings; to *Messenger-Journal* publisher Bob Welch and *Bend of the River* historical magazine publisher Lee Raizk for printing the original descriptions (now reduced largely to manageable captions); to Way Public Library, which permitted me to paw disruptively through and select from their file of photographs; to Lee Gagle, who scanned the 210 images for this book; to the Toledo-Lucas County Library; Wurzell Photography and Video; Christina Lawless; Katherine Hess and Lucille Thornton Pitney for the use of photographs; to the anonymous donor who paid for my photographer son Bill's trip home from Santa Barbara (he donated a week of his time to picture taking); to Judith Justus, Jack Ahern, and my wife Mary for their kind help in copy and proof reading; and to the Board of Directors of Historic Perrysburg, Inc., who encouraged this entire project and who hopes it will be a boost to their long-time commitment to draw attention to and protect this community's built environment.

AN ACT OF CONGRESS

"Be it enacted, etc. That so much of the tract of land twelve miles square, at the 'British fort of the Miami of the Lake at the Foot of The Rapids', ceded by the Wyandot, Delaware, Shawnee, Eel River, Ottawa, Chippewa, Potawatamie, Miami, Weeas, Kickapoo, Plankashaw and Kaskaskia tribes of Indians to the United States by the Treaty of Greenville, on the Third of August, 1795, under the direction of the Surveyor General, be laid off into town lots, streets and avenues, and into out-lots, in such manner and of such dimensions as he may judge proper.

"And be it further enacted, that previously to the disposal at public sale of the before mentioned tract of land, the Surveyor General shall, and he is hereby directed to resurvey, mark the exterior lines of the said tract conformably to the survey made in December, 1805, and also to cause divisional lines to be run through each section and fractional section binding on the said river, so that each subdivision may contain, as early as may be, 16 acres each. And in like manner to cause the "Great Island", lying at the foot of the rapids, in the said river, to be surveyed, and by lines running north and south, to divide the same, as nearly as may be, into six equal parts."

The above is the resolution by the U.S. Congress that was approved April 27, 1816, creating the City of Perrysburg, Ohio. The town was to be about one mile square and platted into town lots of one-quarter acre, with larger "outlots." It was named by Connecticut native Amos Spafford, who in 1810 was named the collector of the port of Miami. (The word Miami was later pronounced and spelled Maumee.)

INTRODUCTION

As is typical in river towns, many of the first and best Perrysburg homes are built on high ground along the waterfront—in our case, mostly along Front and Second, two parallel streets that run the width of town and within which are many high-style architectural examples. The almost irreplaceable craftsmanship in brick and wood in these houses is hard to find elsewhere in such a concentration in a small Midwestern city. It is worth noting that most of them were built when this was a village of 2,000 people or less.

We admittedly stretch a point in assigning a style to many of the buildings shown here simply because they display one or two general characteristics of a particular style. But we do it to help draw attention to architectural elements. Speaking of which, this book is not intended as an architectural text or reference (or would it qualify as such), nor is it in any way a history of Perrysburg. More simply, it is created to give the reader a quick and better appreciation of the area's built environment and the people who created it, plus just enough local history to show what was going on during the time of its creation and development.

That environment can be said to reflect two periods of time: first, westward movement of, in our case, settlers mostly from the Middle Atlantic states (plus immigrants from southern Germany) in the 19th century, during which they left what has been called a textbook of architectural styles (mostly Victorian); and second, the immediate post-World War I period when a number of Toledo's most prominent families chose Perrysburg's side of the Maumee River to seemingly compete in building the most elegant baronial residences.

It should be said that most of the best old buildings in the city survive not only because they were well designed and built, but because their preservation and maintenance has been assured by inclusion in a National Register historic district re-enforced by a historic zoning ordinance and design-review process. The latter controls exterior alterations, demolition, and new building in the district and seems to encourage the community's general interest in and support of preserving Perrysburg's unique character.

About Perrysburg, almost without exception, towns and cities come to be because of their surroundings or some particular natural asset. That was the case with Perrysburg—interestingly enough, by government edict. Following Gen. Anthony Wayne's defeat of the American Indians at the battle of Fallen Timbers across the river in 1794, the tribes ceded a 12-mile square of land pretty well centered on the "foot of the rapids," the shallow water between what is now Perrysburg and its sister community, Maumee. This site is located some 15 miles upriver from Lake Erie and is as far as you can come by boat on open water, stretching all the way from western New York state. After a few miles of shallow rapids, cargoes and travelers of years ago could resume open water travel for a hundred miles west and on south to the Ohio and Mississippi Rivers. The Maumee River's historic travel importance was underscored by the once nearly impassable Great Black Swamp that bordered it all the way to Indiana and extended some 40 miles south.

On both sides of the river, the rapids here were a key spot for, most likely, Native Americans, and most definitely for French, then British, then American traders with the American Indians. It was here that the U.S. government envisioned a busy Great Lakes distribution center for goods consigned to the interior in exchange for furs, hides, and dried meats. And for many years, it served that purpose, even becoming at one time third only to Buffalo and Cleveland ports in goods shipped.

By 1810, about 70 families were living on this side of the river rapids, generally at the foot of and east of the bluff upon which Fort Meigs was to be built, but when the War of 1812 broke out, they fled when British troops and their American Indian allies came here from Detroit and burned the settlement. At the end of the war, the settlers returned and rebuilt, informally calling the place Orleans, or Orleans of the North, perhaps daring to hope that it might one day to some extent be a northern New Orleans.

In 1816, the United States, by an act of Congress, directed the creation of a town a mile down river on higher ground and sent a team of men to survey and lay it out. This is a government action Perrysburg proudly shares with the creation of Washington, D.C. During the early 1820s, and especially after several damaging floods, Orleans inhabitants moved to this higher ground, and their settlement ceased to exist.

The generally agreed-upon founder of this town, certainly one of the first officially established in Northwest Ohio, was Amos Spafford, a New Englander who helped survey what became Cleveland and who came here as collector and postmaster of what was then called the Port of Miami of Lake Erie. Spafford was also the first official land owner in Wood County and the man who named Perrysburg in honor of Oliver Hazard Perry, the hero of the Battle of Lake Erie, which took place not far from here.

This book is the outgrowth of a now 15-year continuing project during which Historic Perrysburg, Inc., a volunteer preservation group, has brought to the public's attention structures in town that are of architectural or historical interest. This has been in the form of literature and monthly articles printed in the Perrysburg *Messenger-Journal* and *Bend of the River*, a magazine on Perrysburg and Toledo area history.

Concentration is on the exterior of the buildings described and the detailing that identifies them with a particular style. Secondary public records were used in most cases to identify original owners and the year of construction, and when best available evidence is inaccurate, we apologize and request that known facts be shared with the author.

One
1820–1830

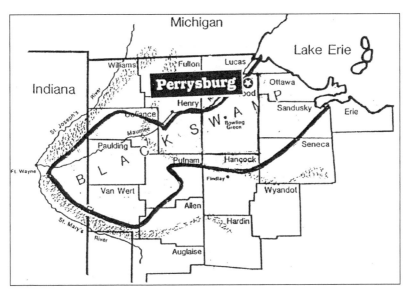

The Great Black Swamp, a dismal almost uninhabitable wilderness and the last place in Ohio to be settled, once extended right up to Perrysburg's present city limits. But it was here on both sides of the foot of the rapids of the Maumee River that white civilization, first the French, then the British, and finally the Americans, probably got a start in this part of the Northwest Territory. It was a natural trade site and an important gate to the interior of the Midwest.

The town's unusual heritage of buildings reaches back almost 185 years and reflects the architectural tastes of eastern United States culture from which many early residents came. Our very first structures range from the first log cabin to John Hollister's unusually elegant home built in 1823. The earliest Perrysburg settlers recorded in letters that the first frame house on this side of the river was built by a David W. Hawley in 1817. He had reportedly brought the finished lumber by boat. The house, no longer existing, was located on the river flats at the end of what would be the northbound extension of West Boundary Street. One traveler wrote that there was not a single house on any of the in-lots (between Mulberry and Hickory, and Front and Seventh), but there were a few log cabins on some of the out-lots extending on to the three Boundary-named streets. A few roads were cut through the forest to furnish logs for a two-story county courthouse and the framework for houses-to-be, a number of which stand today but started as log structures

Nationally, we began flexing our muscles with the Monroe Doctrine opposing European intervention in the Americas, and the canal era emerged with the opening of the Erie Canal between New York City and Lake Erie. Shortly after Perrysburg was platted by the U.S. government in 1816, this area was a part of Logan County nearly 100 miles south of here. In 1820, Wood County was created, and by 1823, the town was about to spring to life, having been named the county seat despite numbering fewer than 200 inhabitants.

FIRST COURTHOUSE ON FIRST BLOCK OF WEST FRONT (BUILT IN 1823). Perrysburg's earliest buildings were made of abundantly available logs. This is a depiction of the first Wood County courthouse built by Daniel Hubbell and Guy Nearing and used as such for 14 years. It was located about 200 feet west of Louisiana Avenue on the south side of West Front Street next door to what was to be the site of the Exchange Hotel, built in the same year (see page 14). Logs were of hand-hewn oak 24 by 32 feet in size. Finished lumber was milled in Monclova, and bricks for the chimney were made at Hubbell's brickworks across the river. The building had offices on the first floor and the courtroom on the second, reached by an outside stairway not shown in this sketch. A log jail, in use until 1847, was moved here and located behind the courthouse. It was enlarged to include foot-square wall and floor timbers secured by pins. Windows consisted of mere slits in the logs. All of this construction cost more than the money on hand, so contractors were paid off with town lots valued at $12 each.

WOOLFERT CABIN AT 577 EAST FRONT (BUILDING DATE UNKNOWN). Whether it is indeed some 200 years old, as once claimed by a Toledo newspaper, this restored two-story log house is typical of the earliest houses. It sat for years on an East River Road bluff less than half a mile outside of town but was moved to the 577 Foundation for educational purposes. It may have originated on a nearby farm along what is now Ford Road. A family of 11 once occupied the place.

POWELL HOUSE AT 538 WEST FRONT (BUILT IN EARLY 1820S). It is not certain who built this small house that is believed to have started as a log cabin. It is traditionally associated with Thomas W. Powell, who came from Utica, New York, as a school teacher in 1820 and who owned the property from 1825 to 1827. He was admitted to the bar and was Wood County prosecuting attorney for 10 years before leaving in 1830. The house has such Greek Revival features as a frieze board and side pilasters. A front porch was removed in recent years, and the right side of the structure could be a later addition.

SECOND POWELL HOUSE AT 300 WEST SECOND (BUILT C. 1829). This Greek Revival house is also attributed to Thomas Powell and is called a fine example of a small "two over two"-room residence, discounting the two wings probably added later. The street-facing gable features plain entablature along the sides, and the chimney extends through the center of the roof ridge. In 1976, the house was completely restored by the Frank Hirst family, with the original interior woodwork and molding retained. Many of the windows contain original panes.

JOHN HOLLISTER HOUSE AT 125 EAST FRONT (BUILT IN 1823). John Hollister, an early and prominent settler, chose the property directly east of the foot of Louisiana Avenue for his house, which for years was a showplace of the northwestern Ohio frontier. While it preceded the Second Empire style, it has its most common similarity, the distinctive mansard roof with dormer windows. A tall cupola with three windows originally topped the roof, and a wide porch in the rear offered a fine view of the river. Hollister was a forwarding and commission merchant, the owner of a line of steamboats, a judge, a postmaster, a mayor, and a member of the Ohio legislature. Presidential candidate William H. Harrison addressed a crowd in front of the residence in 1840, and over the years well into the 20th century, the place saw visitors such as Daniel Webster, William McKinley, Warren Harding, and Nicholas Longworth. The home was destroyed by fire in 1940. (*below*) This photograph, date unknown, shows changes made over time in the Hollister house above before it burned.

SPINK HOUSE AT 503 WEST FRONT (BUILT C. 1827). The latest research shows that this property was never owned by John C. Spink, with whom its name is associated, and that it may not be as old as thought. But we will let stand its long-time identity. It is perched on the side of Indian Hill where warriors are said to have camped before joining in the sieges of Fort Meigs. Its Greek Revival features include a centered doorway surrounded by multi-paned sidelights and a transom topped by an entablature supported by pilasters. That it was once the old Customs House, an Underground Railroad station, and a stagecoach stop is probably apocryphal—though in the 1920s, it was known to be used for the Sunnyside Tea Room.

AURORA SPAFFORD HOUSE AT 27340 WEST RIVER ROAD (BUILT IN 1820S). Built by the son of town founder Amos Spafford, this simple Greek Revival house is called a "half house" (two and a half rooms deep with a Shaker-type interior) by the Ohio Historical Society. Now on the National Register, the house was moved a few feet from its original foundation during restoration by the current owner. Otherwise, it appears unaltered, but there are plans for change. It was the meeting place in the 1820s for the area Methodist congregation.

EXCHANGE HOTEL AT 140 WEST FRONT (BUILT IN 1823). (*above*) This famous old hostelry was built by Samuel Spafford, another son of Amos Spafford, for John Hollister. It was later bought and operated by Samuel's son, Jarvis. Built of walnut logs and later covered with clapboard, it was the social center of the community for several generations. Among the guests and visitors over its 84 years in business were Pres. James K. Polk, Gen. Winfield Scott, Daniel Webster, Peter Navarre, and assorted national and state congressmen, governors, and judges who could enjoy a view of the busy Maumee River across the street. Political gatherings and veterans' reunions over the years used its 25 rooms that extended to the rear, and locals attended the festivals, balls, concerts, wedding receptions, and even lawn croquet games staged there. (*below*) Today the original framework still exists, but all vestiges of the former Exchange Hotel are gone. Following a fire in 1907, the structure was altered to a two-family dwelling and is now a commercial building with apartments.

Two

1830–1840

This was an exciting decade in Perrysburg. Wooden ships and boats were still the primary means of travel and commerce, and this area had the raw material to build them.

The shipbuilding industry here was centered along the flats of the river, and larger and larger vessels were being constructed—sailing schooners, steam-driven side-wheelers, and propeller steamboats, some up to nearly 700 tons. Not only that—with its natural trading center at the foot of the rapids, Perrysburg was one of the busiest ports on Lake Erie, and the Miami Canal from Cincinnati to Dayton was extended to the Maumee River, and work began on the Wabash and Erie and Miami-Erie Canal links to the lake.

Road access to Perrysburg was improving (barely) with the state putting a macadam, or stone, surface on the east-west Maumee and Western Reserve Road (now Route 20) across the swamp, though it was still an almost impassable bog during wet weather. The first short-lived log bridge was built across the river between here and Maumee.

Our town was chartered by the Ohio General Assembly and grew to over a thousand people. With that came election of John C. Spink, the first mayor. After one of many fires that defied bucket brigades and destroyed frame homes and business buildings, village council passed an ordinance creating our first volunteer fire department. But success still mostly depended on the availability of nearby water.

In 1838, work began to replace the first log county courthouse, and a Greek Revival-style structure took shape on the site of today's municipal buildings. It was to be six years before the structure was completed. If there was any dampener to this progress, it might have been the so-called "Toledo War," when Ohio and Michigan quarreled over the state line and militia from both sides threatened one another from across the river. However, residents were said to have been thrilled over Ohio troops headquartered in town and drilling in our streets, with Governor Robert Lucas as commander.

AMOS SPAFFORD II HOUSE AT 347 EAST SECOND (BUILT IN THE 1830S). Records suggest that the grandson of the town's founder built this small, neat Greek Revival house. Hand-hewn lumber can be seen held together by square nails, along with two-inch walnut sheathing material. Spafford died in California during the gold rush, and the property was bought by Jesup W. Scott, who founded and co-edited the first newspaper here and in the Maumee Valley. He later became editor of the *Toledo Blade* and a founder of the University of Toledo.

PHOENIX BLOCK AT 128–130 LOUISIANA (BUILT IN 1830S). One of the oldest downtown business buildings is this Federal-style built for Joseph Creps's Eagle Hotel, later called the Baird House, and still later the Franklin House. In 1858, it was remodeled for a general business building, and in 1871, an interior wall divided the first floor down the middle. The Kazmaier grocery occupied half of it for 60 years. Because of the swamp then, cellars were not practical, and even today a ramp leads up into the building.

A. M. THOMPSON HOUSE AT 223–225 WEST SECOND (BUILT IN 1830S). A much altered home of Italianate style, the A. M. Thompson house features a two-story angled bay with windows topped by segmental arches of vertically angled brick over protruding brick sills. In 1928, a two-story frame addition was made in the rear. A frame entrance and the porch on the right side are also additions. Thompson was a dry goods and grocery merchant and farmer and was active in civic affairs.

LINDSAY HOUSE AT 348 WEST FRONT (BUILT IN 1836). This is a comparatively small Greek Revival-style house with an attractive off-center entrance surrounded by sidelights and transom. The windows have stone lintels. Frame extensions were later added to the left and rear sides. Lindsay operated a sash, door, and blind factory along the river and was married to Sarah McKnight, daughter of one of the first families to make their home here.

CRANKER HOUSE AT 310 WEST SECOND (BUILT IN 1830S). This Greek Revival-style home was likely built by Ruben Sawyer, though it is identified more with the Peter Cranker family. Typical Greek details include the wide trim band or frieze board under the eaves, multi-glazed windows, and the front door with classical sidelights and transom. Little is known of Sawyer, but Cranker was a well-known wagon, carriage, and sleigh maker.

PETER CRANKER. Cranker was a former village councilman who began as a blacksmith and ended as a wagon and carriage maker.

WAY HOUSE AT 529 HICKORY (BUILT IN 1830S). Believed to be built by a John Chambers, this house was the Willard V. Way family house for many years, and it once stood on the corner of Indiana and Walnut where the fire department is now. Way came here from New York state and was a prominent lawyer, county prosecutor, mayor, and civic leader, but was considered by some to be rather miserly by nature. Upon his death, they were surprised to learn that he left the village money to build a library and to buy books, six lots for a park, his house, and funds for a school scholarship. The house was moved in the early 1900s.

WAY HOUSE AT ORIGINAL LOCATION ON SOUTHEAST CORNER OF INDIANA AND WALNUT. The lady in this undated photograph is believed to be Mrs. Eugenie Chapman, a schoolteacher.

YEAGER HOUSE AT 343 WEST INDIANA (BUILT IN 1830S). German immigrant John J. Yeager owned this house from the 1840s, and his descendants lived in it until 1990. A Greek Revival temple-style farm house, it stood on the then outskirts of town. Other than the wing on the right, it has had minimal changes. Two of Yeager's descendants served as mayors of Perrysburg, and one was a long-time merchant.

EARLIER PHOTOGRAPH OF YEAGER HOUSE. This undated photograph shows what the house looked like before the present embellishments.

B. F. HOLLISTER HOUSE AT 407 WEST FRONT (BUILT IN 1830S). Benjamin Hollister, from Massachusetts, built this house whose roofline and elliptical fanlight in the gable reflect the earlier Federal period. It has a framework of hand-hewn timbers secured by mortise and tenon joints and wide-plank pine floors laid directly over logs. Hollister (brother of John, see page 12) ran a general store and was in the fur trade with the American Indians. He escorted parts of the Ottawa and Miami tribes to their exile in the west.

ROBY HOUSE AT 76 LOCUST (BELIEVED BUILT IN 1830S). This house was built in the Greek Revival style around an older house or cabin that could have been a Native American trading post. Charles Roby probably built some early part of this version after buying it in about 1836. Once a merchant, Roby became captain of the steamship *G. P. Griffith*, which on its maiden voyage in 1850 burned and sank in Lake Erie with the loss of almost 300 people. It remains Lake Erie's single worst tragedy.

STONE HOUSE AT 425 EAST SECOND (BUILT IN 1830S). Little is known of Enos Stone, believed to be the builder of this Greek Revival home with the off-center entrance, sidelights, and a three-pane transom. Notice the tall and narrow windows with slightly pedimental moldings, and the wide roof overhang. Alterations include an addition with a shed roof and a glass-walled sunroom in the rear and a screened porch on the right side.

BINGHAM-FOLEY HOUSE AT 80 LOCUST (BUILT IN 1836). Much altered and added to, this Greek Revival home began as a square one-story dwelling with a hipped roof over four rooms. In one change, the main entrance was moved to the left side and the two-story section added. Joseph J. Bingham was a forwarding and commission merchant, and Dr. Norman J. Foley, who did much of the additions, was a leading thyroid surgeon here and in Toledo.

Three
1840–1850

The biggest local happening of the decade was the political rally in 1840 when presidential Whig candidate William Henry Harrison returned to the site of his military victory during the War of 1812. According to reports of the time, this attracted between 25,000 and 60,000 people, who came by boat from east and west, and by wagon and carriage from all directions to flood Perrysburg and the old Fort Meigs battleground. Harrison was the houseguest of John Hollister, from whose spacious front yard along Front Street he addressed a throng of supporters. Throughout the country, this campaign was reported to be the liveliest in the nation's history, with dancing in the streets, log cabin songs, hard-cider ditties, and marches. Harrison ran his campaign from a log cabin built atop a wagon bed to which was attached a barrel of cider. Perrysburg's annual celebration of the rally usually includes a similar parade float.

Perrysburg continued to prosper. From the foot of Louisiana Avenue to some five miles upriver, a huge ditch was dug along the river's edge, and water diverted into it flowed downstream and over a waterwheel, which put into motion machinery driven by leather belts. It was the Hydraulic Canal, paid for by the taxpayers, and before electricity was available, the source of power for local industry. With it came our first small manufacturing firms that required it for grinding, sawing, and cutting.

Our first school building was erected as a frame structure with a bell tower—the pride of the community. A covered bridge across the river replaced the first less-substantial log bridge, which washed away in a flood. There were no less than 5 hotels serving this busy county seat of about 1,500 people. Methodist, Evangelical, Baptist, and Universalist congregations were now worshipping in their own church buildings, while Presbyterians used other facilities, and Catholics crossed the river to Maumee

Beach House at 342 West Second (Built in 1838). This Greek Revival house was probably not built with the wing on the right, but the original portion shows the pediment in the front gable and wide frieze board, six-pane window glazing, and front entrance with side pilasters. Gilbert Beach, from New York state, was a long-time grocer, dry goods merchant, and community leader. The house has a foundation two-and-a-half-feet thick and was once heated by seven fireplaces.

Second Beach House at 232 West Second (Built c. 1840). This is one of several similarly shaped homes in town commonly called saltbox houses. It is not certain who built it, but it is also generally attributed to Gilbert Beach (discussed above). The shape derives from the practice in Colonial days of simply continuing the roof slope over added space, giving it an early American saltbox shape. The front entrance here is topped with a small pediment and framed by simple pilasters.

HALSTED HOUSE AT 125 EAST FRONT (BUILT IN 1940). When the then 117-year-old John Hollister House (see page 12) was destroyed by fire in 1940, owners Mr. and Mrs. John Halsted commissioned local architect Donald M. Buckhout to design this Second French Empire version of the original. He replicated many of the features of the original structure. It is laid out in a series of connecting wings, with a large garage on the right side with living quarters above it. The garage is connected to the house by a long, attractive, curved Doric colonnaded pergola. This replaced the original porte-cochere, or covered carriage entrance.

PERGOLA AND GARAGE OF THE HALSTED PROPERTY. John Halsted, who grew up in Toledo, was a broker and real estate executive. He served in the navy during World War II and died during the 1960s.

SHEPLER HOUSE AT 116 WEST SECOND (BUILT C. 1840). The builder of this Greek Revival house just around the corner off our main street is not known, but it is identified as that of the Shepler family who lived there for over 70 years. Shepler was an innkeeper. Now hemmed in by other commercial buildings, the building was once a stand-alone front-gabled residence. The wood framing in the house is said to resemble the very old post-and-girt system, employing oak lumber.

BLOOMFIELD HOUSE AT 233 EAST SECOND (BUILT IN 1840S). This Greek Revival-style house started as a one-and-a-half-story building. Among other additions over the years were the one-story room with a shed roof on the right side, a small front entrance porch, small porches at the rear and left sides, and an extension with a flat roof in the rear. It was built by Edmund Bloomfield, who once taught school, was a skilled carpenter who worked in a Toledo shipyard, and was one of our county commissioners.

SPAFFORD HOUSE AT 514 WEST FRONT (BUILT C. 1840). This temple-style Greek Revival house has long been associated with the James and Jarvis Spafford families, grandsons of the town's founder. Jarvis Spafford ran the Exchange Hotel (see page 14). He and two of his young children died in the 1854 cholera epidemic. Little is known of James, who later lived in the hotel, but their sister Mary Spafford was born in one of the abandoned Fort Meigs blockhouses, which had been temporarily occupied immediately following the end of the War of 1812. Their earlier family home had been burned by the British and American Indians during the war.

FRONT VIEW OF SPAFFORD HOUSE. This typical Greek Revival building has interrupted or return cornice lines, five six-over-six windows, and a centered entrance topped by a ten-pane transom and flanked by sidelights.

SECOND COURTHOUSE AT WALNUT AND INDIANA (BUILT C. 1840). Begun in the late 1830s, this 50 by 70-foot brick building was Wood County's second courthouse for 30 years. Of classical Greek Revival design, favored for public buildings, this one featured four large two-story Doric columns in the front and a tower topped with a dome. It was described at the time as "Roman Doric of bascilican [an oblong shape] style" and was built by Loomis Brigham and Jarius Curtis over a period of about six years and at a cost of $20,000. In 1872, fire broke out in a cooper's shop a couple of blocks west of Louisiana between Indiana and Third where about two acres of ground were covered with barrel staves and other wood combustibles. That was brought under control after the shop and two nearby houses were destroyed, but a steady wind revived the fire overnight and the next morning a nearby barn caught fire, then another dwelling, and embers from those fell on the unoccupied courthouse, which burned to the ground. At that time, not even a hand-pulled fire engine was owned by the village.

H. P. Averill House at 345 East Front (Built in 1846). A native of Hartford, Connecticut, Henry Averill came here in 1844 and was a partner with his brother-in-law Dr. Erasmus D. Peck in the Peck & Averill Flour Mill that served a large portion of surrounding counties. It was located on the waterfront near the foot of Louisiana Avenue. Although containing elements of the Federal style, the house is clearly Greek Revival with a front gable pediment (repeated over the door), tall, narrow windows, and wide corner pilasters resembling Greek columns. The elliptical fanlight in the pediment is one of several in town. Interior woodwork is particularly noteworthy for architectural details. There have been many additions to the rear of this house over the years.

H. P. Averill House Pilasters. Extra-wide corner pilasters are a feature of this fine old house.

WEBB HOUSE AT 224 WEST FRONT (BUILT IN 1843). This house was built by John C. Webb, who came here in 1820 and was later Wood County's sheriff. The front-gabled house has tall, fluted corner pilasters associated with Greek Revival structures and a large second-story side porch (probably an addition) with a balustrade supported by square columns that echo the pilasters. The shallow roof is at least partially supported by square original bark-covered round logs without a ridge beam. Webb, born in New York City, temporarily "squatted" with his family in an abandoned house near the river before buying land to house his hat-making factory.

JOHN C. WEBB. Some sources say the Webb family was the first to inhabit the area until 1823. Mr. Webb had a lifetime of 90 years, during which he was married 3 times and fathered 18 children.

WITZLER BUILDING AT 116 LOUISIANA (PROBABLY BUILT IN 1840s). *(right)* Charles Witzler owned this building in 1895, but it, or an earlier version, predates that by at least half a century. It is commercial Italianate in style and was described as of unpainted brick with contrasting black window frames. A dentiled cornice divides the first and second floor facade, and the top features fluted brackets, dentils, and square tin rosettes, all originally light or white colored, and three trios of small rectangular windows. Charles Witzler manufactured bed springs and later moved a furniture and undertaking business into this building. It was the beginning of the Witzler Funeral Home business operated by that family for nearly 70 years. The small frame building on the left (still standing but with a partial brick facade) was the John C. Spink home, later the town's first public library, which was still later expanded into the Witzler building. *(left)* For many years, this building housed a "5¢ and 10¢" store. At this writing, it is an antique shop, but is slated for a new occupant.

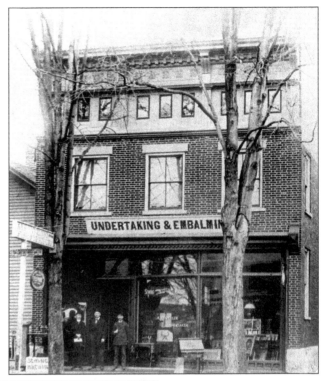

PERRIN HOUSE AT 510 WEST FRONT (BUILT C. 1845). This highly ornamental Gothic Revival house was constructed by Pennsylvanian Jonathan Perrin, a builder himself when he arrived in 1827. The steep gable roof with curvilinear vergeboards and decorative finials and pendants at the top are eye-catchers. Six-pane windows with Gothic molding and ogee arches are in the front gable and eight paned windows in the secondary gables. In 1929, Toledo architects Britsch and Munger remodeled part of the exterior, adding dormers and the side entrance on the left. (*below*) Delicate details include the ogee arch on this window, the finial atop the gable representing a pineapple (symbol of hospitality), and the pendant beneath it depicting an acorn, a popular motif in the Gothic tradition.

FORMER EVANGELICAL CHURCH AT 331 EAST SECOND (BUILT IN 1846). (*above*) Now the Marantha Chapel of the Pentacostal Church of God, this building holds the record (159 years) for unbroken longevity as a Perrysburg house of worship. It began as Grace Evangelical Church, built by member Jacob Hufford (spelled "Hoffert" on his tombstone), who supplied timber from his own property. Rooms and extensions have been added over the years. The denomination united with Grace United Methodist Church and now worships in their building on East Boundary. (*below*) The congregation of Grace Evangelical assembled for this undated photograph.

PARKS HOUSE AT 246 WEST SECOND (BUILT C. 1847). Minus additions to the rear, this classically proportioned and well-maintained Greek Revival house was built by Pennsylvanian James J. Parks, who came here as a shoe and harness maker and became a prosperous and well-known businessman and justice of the peace. The front-gabled roof, wide frieze board, and matching pediment over the entrance are all typical of the style. Pilasters at the facade corners balance the gable pediment. The house was restored in 1938 under supervision of local architect Donald Buckhout.

PARKS HOUSE ENTRANCE. The entrance has a miniature entablature and Doric-capped pilasters. A ten-pane transom and four-pane sidelights surround the door.

OLD COUNTY JAIL AT 240 WEST INDIANA (BUILT IN 1847). The first Wood County jail was of logs and sat by the log courthouse on West Front Street (see page 10). This jail by comparison was a fortress. The frame is of walnut hand-hewn beams with rafters and joints mortised and pinned with wooden pegs. The walls are four layers of small brick, and in the first floor confinement area, the walls and floors are of stone blocks two feet thick. There were six 5 by 6-foot cells, and upstairs the dangerously insane were confined. It was discontinued as a county facility in 1870 but used as the village jail until about 1900. The Charles Hoffmann Sr. family acquired the structure (now on the National Register) in 1957 and converted it into a three-apartment building.

OLDEST CIVIC BUILDING. This undated photograph was taken while the building was still a jail. An unknown architect was paid $15 for designing and supervising its construction.

CARRANOR HUNT & POLO CLUB AT 502 EAST SECOND (BUILT IN 1848). The right front of this rambling building was built as a home by Nathaniel Blinn for his son, Doan. The style is Greek Revival with the typical pediment, broad fascia, and corner pilasters. The parlor, with impressive floor-to-ceiling woodwork, is the only part of the interior still unaltered. The elder Blinn was a contractor on the Maumee and Western Reserve Road (Route 20). He served as a village councilman and a county judge. The building was purchased for the newly organized club in 1923.

CARRANOR DEPOT. Slated to be torn down in 1970, the depot (then located at Third and Louisiana) was acquired by the club with the help of member John Biggers, a former director of the B&O Railroad. It was moved to the club property where it is used primarily by platform tennis players as a warming place between games.

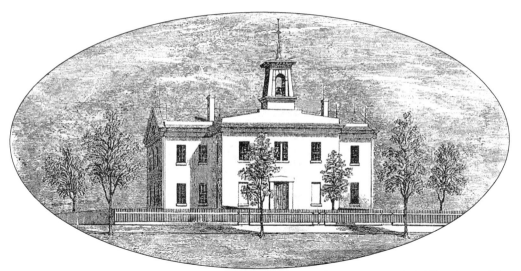

FIRST SCHOOL BUILDING AT LOUISIANA AND INDIANA (BUILT IN 1849). The first public school building in town was this two-story frame, 60 by 90 feet in size. Albert D. Wright, who was to die in the cholera epidemic 5 years later, was the first superintendent of Union School, with 50 enrolled pupils. Three young women were the first high school graduates.

SECOND SCHOOL. In 1868, nearly 20 years after it was built, the original structure above was enlarged and drastically remodeled to this version—3 stories, a new bell tower, and brick outer walls. It had six classrooms, a laboratory, an office, and two recitation rooms. In 1894, the school burned down. Rebuilding began quickly, and classes continued in Town Hall (see page 68).

THIRD SCHOOL. (*above*) At a cost of some $30,000, this handsome Richardsonian Romanesque building, designed by Arthur Hitchcock, a local architect with Toledo's Bacon & Huber, became our third public school in 1894. Typical features are the large square 80-foot-high tower and rounded arches at the entrance and in some windows. It was at first heated by coal, and drinking water came from a well outside in the front. An auditorium with theater-like seats was a useful added community asset. (*below*) Wear, tear, and wind resulted in this present version created in 1954, with the bell tower and entire third floor removed.

Four

1850–1860

Overshadowed by a growing Toledo—with its deeper river water—Perrysburg diminished in importance as a port. Like most ambitious communities of the day, it did everything possible to encourage growth, including helping pay for construction to get a railroad—eventually succeeding in about 1858. In time, there were double tracks with passenger and freight trains running at all hours, and a two-story depot and large engine house on Third Street. In addition, new telegraph service in town opened the era of broader communication with the outside world.

Many of our better old homes were built at this time, as locally-made brick was easily available. Stagecoach service to Findlay used a plank-covered road created by area investors, and there was daily boat service to Toledo. A foundry, tannery, woolen factory, and flour mill were among river-front industries.

Among 2.5 million immigrants entering the United States during this decade were a number who came here from the same region of Germany. They were hard-working Catholic families whose names are still prominent today. And the hope of sudden wealth lured several Perrysburg men to seek California gold.

Two great tragedies marred these years. In 1850, this community grieved the loss of the entire Capt. Charles C. Roby family (and relatives of another Perrysburg family), along with the crew and some 250 mostly-immigrant passengers on Capt. Roby's new lake steamer, G. P. Griffith, which on its maiden voyage burned and sank. And in 1854, during a 7-week summer period, a deadly cholera epidemic claimed possibly upwards of 200 Perrysburg area residents. It is believed to have reached here when a child brought to Perrysburg from East Toledo died of the disease on July 3. The next day, when people celebrated the Fourth of July with an all-day picnic and attended a ball that evening, it spread, and within a few days, over half of the nearly 1800 people then living here fled town.

EBERLY HOUSE AT 216 EAST SECOND (BUILT C. 1850). The original frame portion of this house was built by boot and shoe tradesman John Eberly who came here from Germany. The front of the one-story left wing (probably added) is of brick, said to have replaced a wooden wall damaged in a fire. The front entrance is flanked by four-paned sidelights above which is a full entablature. Eberly built the brick business building on the corner of Louisiana and Second for his hand-made boot and shoe business. (see page 59).

JOSIAH MILLER HOUSE AT 422 EAST SECOND (BUILT C. 1850). This house began as a simple Greek Revival home, but remodeling in the early 1900s added Colonial Revival features such as the three gabled dormers that echo the pediment over the front door. There is a wide frieze board and massive wrap-around pilasters at the corners, topped by Doric-style capitals. Miller was a well-known carpenter who came here from Connecticut in about 1835. He was once a county commissioner and township trustee.

J. M. Hall House at 315 East Front (Built c. 1850). This is another showcase example of Italianate architecture. Built by James Manning Hall, a dry goods and grocery merchant, postmaster, and civic leader, it has iron cresting on the roof, a very wide frieze board with windows, paired brackets under the eaves, narrow windows, and two-story bays on both sides, with carved stone lintels—all typical of the style. The semi-circlular portico was added in the 1930s.

Frieze Board Windows. The windows between double brackets are covered in metal fretwork and provide light for the attic area.

J. A. HALL HOUSE AT 321 EAST SECOND (BUILT C. 1850). Jarius Augustus Hall, with his brother James M., operated a general store at Louisiana and Front. They came from Vermont, and J. A. built the original part of this temple-style Greek Revival house featuring a strong pediment over a wide frieze board, six-over-six windows, and corner pilasters. The large side yard, on part of which the added wing now sits, was an orchard, and it is said that an originally planted Osage Orange hedge (resistant to free-grazing livestock) still defines some of the property line.

J. A. HALL HOUSE FRONT ENTRANCE. This is one of our better examples of a classical Greek Revival front entrance flanked by pilasters with inlaid fretwork and capped by a complete entablature.

JOHN HOOD HOUSE AT 377 WEST SECOND (BUILT C. 1850S). The two side portions could be additions to this modest home of a retired immigrant farmer from Scotland. The builder is unknown. Unfinished log beams with bark on them certify its old age. Hood seemed to have prospered, but he lived rather frugally. In 1901, he bought the land that is now Hood Park and seeking anonymity, quietly donated it to the village. Probably at his insistence, it was at first known as Monument Park, the site of the area's soldiers and sailors monument.

STUBBS HOUSE AT 326 WEST FRONT (BUILT C. 1853). Originally with "saw-tooth" vergeboards in the front gable, this house, built by James F. Stubbs, possesses some attractive Greek Revival characteristics, especially the recessed front entrance flanked by pilasters and a complete entablature above. Significant additions have been made on the sides and rear. Stubbs came from Cumberland County, Pennsylvania, in 1835 and was a partner with James L. Douglas in a riverfront warehouse when Perrysburg was a busy lake port.

HOUSTON HOUSE AT 420 WEST FRONT (BUILT C. 1850). This large, frequently added-to house has Greek Revival and Italianate features. The original portion was probably built by William Houston. The roof has a very shallow slope with Italianate-style brackets. The main entrance, redone at some point, has unusual carved brackets that flank a heavy oak door with sidelights. A large former barn is joined to the rear by a breezeway. William Houston was a strong abolitionist and once owned a commercial building on the site of Hood Park that was said to be an Underground Railroad station (see page 49).

FORMER HOUSTON HOUSE BARN. The former barn, now painted white, adjoins the rear of the house. It was moved there in the early 1940s from across town. Schools were closed so students could watch, and the daily train schedule was altered for the move.

SMITH HOUSE AT 138 WEST FIFTH (BUILT IN 1853). This Greek Revival house was built by Pennsylvanian Addison Smith, who came here to visit his sister in 1832 and stayed. He spent some time in the mercantile business and over time was our mayor, county auditor, township treasurer, and representative in the Ohio legislature. He was a man of inventive genius, holding more than a dozen patents, including one for a propeller wheel for gunboats that was adopted by the navy.

BATES HOUSE AT 566 EAST FRONT (BUILT C. 1855). This house once sat at what is now the Kazmaier Grocery parking lot on East Second. It is associated with the pioneer John Bates family. Italianate in style, it has typical details such as a symmetrical shape, hipped roof, and wide overhanging eaves. The full porch is supported by slender posts with scrolled brackets. John Bates came here in 1835 and was a long-time Wood County treasurer and township trustee.

NORTON HOUSE AT 402 EAST FRONT (BUILT C. 1855). This brick house has an interesting blend of Victorian features that include gingerbread trim typical of Gothic Revival, tall Italianate-like windows with segmental arches, an extended brick frieze following the gable angles, and a frame bay window containing a row of dentils. Jesse E. Norton started and was cashier of the first bank in town. He served as mayor and was a colonel in the Civil War, in which he was wounded and taken prisoner.

HAZEL FARM HOUSE ON FIVE POINT ROAD (BUILT C. 1850). This nostalgic photograph shows what a typical farm house and front yard in this area looked like a century and a half ago. It was the home of German-born Adam Hazel and was originally a log house sitting on a dry spot in the Black Swamp south of town—although by that time the swamp was being slowly drained. The picture was taken by an itinerant photographer before home cameras were common.

C. A. Hoffman Grocery and Restaurant at 113–115 Louisiana (Built in 1856).
This undated photograph shows the hardware store built by Brown & Hunt, owners of a local foundry of that name, perhaps as a retail outlet for items they made such as cast iron plows, kettles, and stoves. The next owner was Bostwick & Tyler who later moved to Toledo to start the wholesale firm of Bostwick, Braun & Co., one of Toledo's oldest existing firms. It was typical of frame downtown buildings of that time, with living quarters upstairs. The front entrance shows a display of produce, fruit, baskets and tubs, and sacked grain or flour. In 1889, Christopher A. Hoffman bought the building from German immigrant John Schwind, and in 1891, he sold the saloon and restaurant section to his father but continued running the grocery business. They put in steel roofing and a pressed steel ceiling and installed a private water system fed by a well and elevated tank. The building burned down in 1901, and the site is now occupied by the Ammon Building, with the downstairs space currently used by Kids Klothesline.

JAMES HOOD HOUSE AT 202 WEST FIFTH (BUILT C. 1857). (*above*) Built by an immigrant Scotsman, this is another typical temple-style Greek Revival residence. Two and a half stories high, it has a shallow-roof pitch, broad fascia and return gable ends, and a recessed Greek entrance flanked by Doric pilasters and sidelights. James Hood and a brother operated a general store, and he once served as mayor. (*below*) The return cornice and fanlight in the gable of the Hood house are features frequently seen in Perrysburg.

Five

1860–1870

The Perrysburg area supplied its share of men to the Union cause during the Civil War. Nearly 400 served, and records indicate that over 100 were killed or died of disease or accidents. Volunteer infantry companies were raised and led by at least two prominent citizens, and another served as commandant of Fort McHenry in Baltimore. At the very outset, a number of citizens responded to President Lincoln's first call for 75,000 volunteers to put down the southern states' "insurrection"—a state of affairs that soon was to begin 4 years of bloody Civil War. Later about a half dozen of our older civilian men, called "squirrel hunters," answered the call to help protect Cincinnati from threatening rebels.

Population changes had made Bowling Green a more centrally-located site for the Wood County seat, and Bowling Green interests persuaded the Ohio General Assembly to allow a county-wide referendum on the issue. The result was approval of the transfer by a disputed handful of votes, and questions about the honesty of the presentation of the issue touched off a rancorous "Ten Years War" between our two towns that lasted well into the next decade.

Typical of the times, underground help to runaway slaves went undocumented, but one or two "stations" were said to be in town. One of them was said to be the building behind the horse in this photograph in what is now Hood Park. This is likely since two trunk line routes from the south merged in this area. (The man in the photograph is Marshal Frank R Thornton, mentioned on page 104.)

The old frame Union School was bricked over and a third story added. The Presbyterians, Catholics, Lutherans, and German Methodists were worshipping in their own buildings, and among local industries were a paper mill, several stave factories, and a wooden bowl factory. A seasonal industry was the netting of fish in the river with as many as 1,200 bushels processed and shipped 1 year. Civic leaders failed to get the new State Soldiers and Sailors Home located at the Fort Meigs site. It went to Sandusky instead, but over 50 veterans of the Fort Meigs 1813 sieges came for a reunion.

Lt. Col. George A. Custer and his staff dismounted the train here after the Civil War en route to a Texas assignment and were later involved in a battle against American Indians who had earlier captured and murdered local resident Clara Blinn on the Santa Fe Trail.

PECK HOUSE AT 112 EAST SECOND (BUILT C. 1860S). While prominent physician Erasmus D. Peck later lived in the far more opulent home of John Hollister (see page 12), he is believed to have also built and lived in this house. It has a Greek Revival doorway and attractive frieze board, but otherwise it is plain. The tiny building on the right was the barbershop of a later owner. Dr. Peck practiced medicine here for 40 years, was involved in numerous early businesses, was our mayor, and served in the Ohio legislature and the U.S. House of Representatives.

HECKLER HOUSE AT 140 EAST SECOND (BUILT C. 1860S). This is a small vernacular Greek Revival home just around the corner from our main street. It was built by John Heckler Sr. and remained in the family for nearly 85 years. The lace-like scrollwork on the four front porch spindle columns are eye-catching. The left side of the house features a small porch in the same style and a gabled two-story bay. Heckler came from Germany and was the father of seven sons. The wife of one son remained a resident of the house until 1956.

WILLIAM BARTON HOUSE AT 220 EAST SECOND (BUILT C. 1860). Historic inventories suggest that this Greek Revival house was built in the 1860s, but it could have been built later by dry goods merchant William Barton whose family lived in it until 1918. The original symmetrical part of it contains the usual wide frieze board, return cornices, and sidelights and pilaster-like door surround. Barton was an Englishman by birth. He lost 14 relatives en route here from England in the *G. P. Griffith* tragedy (see Roby House, page 21).

JONES HOUSE AT 220 WEST FRONT (BUILT C. 1863). Details in this house suggest Greek Revival, Federal, Georgian, and Italianate architecture. It was built by Elizha Jones. The house has undergone a number of changes, including rear additions and the removal of brackets under the eaves of the hipped roof. Noteworthy features are the box-like shape, multi-paned windows, rather wide frieze board, and the massive broken pediment with a pineapple at its center over the paneled front door, which is framed by pilasters.

CROOK HOUSE AT 502 WEST FRONT (BUILT C. 1864). English-born farmer William Crook came here in 1832. Later, he bought the Baird House (page 16) with his son William Jr. and opened an agricultural implement and undertaking business. Crook built this house with a two-story front-facing bay. An early photograph shows scrollwork at the tops of seven porch columns, double brackets under the eaves, and a white picket fence across the front.

HANNAH HOUSE AT 214 EAST SECOND (BUILT C. 1865). Just off downtown Louisiana Avenue, this house could have been built by a William Hannah, who owned the property for 18 years. The plain vergeboard in the front gable, the overhanging eaves supported by small single brackets, and the single small window in the downstairs facade are among noticeable architectural features. This house served as the Presbyterian Church parsonage for over 85 years.

HUNT HOUSE AT 321 EAST FRONT (BUILT C. 1863). This handsome frame Italianate house was probably built while the owner, Lewis Cass Hunt, was serving as a general in the Civil War. It has a hipped roof with paired incised brackets, and dentils set against a wide frieze board. Bay windows are on both sides, and the portico has the same type roof and brackets, plus Tuscan supporting columns. There is a two-story carriage house in the rear. Hunt was present at Lee's surrender at Appomattox in 1865. His father came through here at the outbreak of the War of 1812 and returned in 1818 to live. The family was related to Lewis Cass, governor of Michigan territory during the so-called Toledo-Michigan War. (*right*) The double front door has beautiful etched glass windows and an etched and wheel-cut transom.

GETZ HOUSE AND STORE AT 115 WEST FRONT (BUILT C. 1865). This brick structure is part of what is commonly known as the old Rheinfrank Hospital, but it originally looked like this when it was the home, grocery, and saloon of the George Getz family. The commercial section was in the rear just above Perrysburg's then riverfront warehouses, mills, and shipping docks. Getz was among a colony of Bavarians who came here in 1852. In 1897, Dr. John H. Rheinfrank (see page 91) had his architect son, George, add a wing and convert the building into a hospital.

OLD RHEINFRANK HOSPITAL. The Getz house and store in the photograph above took on this look after being acquired by Dr. John H. Rheinfrank. With his son William and son-in-law Norman Foley, both thyroid specialists, this small hospital gained fame as a treatment center for thyroid ailments. Today the structure is a commercial building.

FINK HOUSE AT 208 EAST INDIANA (BUILT C. 1865). Shortly after the Civil War, German-born John Fink built this frame Italianate house, which remained in the family until just after World War II. It features attractive gingerbread scrollwork on the front entry, with square supporting porch posts. Most of the windows have wooden pediments. The wing on the east side is likely an addition. Very little is known about John Fink himself.

HIMMELMAN HOUSE AT 215 WEST SECOND (BELIEVED BUILT IN 1860S). This is one of a number of Perrysburg houses whose modern looks belie their true age when you examine the rough-sawn framing. The probable builder was German immigrant and Civil War veteran John C. Himmelman who bought the property in 1866 and sold it seven years later for much more than he paid for it. With numerous alterations since, the original look is lost.

OLD "COURTHOUSE" AT 535 EAST FRONT (BUILT PROBABLY C. 1860S). Its builder and age are lost in time, but this almost miniature Greek Revival structure once sat on the east side of the first block of Louisiana and was the law office of Daniel K. Hollenbeck. Its original size was about 15 by 30 feet. It was sometimes referred to as the "courthouse," possibly because it looks like one with its stately fluted columns, but more likely because it may have been used as one by an early justice of the peace. In 1919, it was bought by Robert C. Pew, a founder of Sun Oil Company, and moved to his estate on Maple Street where it was adapted for use as a studio for his daughter, who was an artist. The floors are of random-width pine attached with wooden pegs, and bark-covered log beams confirm its antiquity. It has been enlarged in the rear for a bedroom. It has also been moved once or twice, and the present owner uses it as a guesthouse.

STRAIN HOUSE AT 332 EAST FRONT (BUILT C. 1865). This house reminds one of a bungalow with its sloping porch columns. A closer look reveals its older Greek Revival heritage with the low pitched roof and interrupted cornice returns and the front-facing gable. The porch, large front picture window, a casement window on the right side, and an extension on the back appear to be additions. The builder is thought to be George Strain, a West Virginia attorney who served as our county prosecutor during the Civil War.

CHAMPNEY HOUSE AT 302 EAST SECOND (BUILT C. 1865). Aaron R. Champney, an Erie, Pennsylvania, native, spent 18 years on the Great Lakes before coming here and becoming a drug store owner. The house is Italianate in style and after years of neglect was recently renovated. The tall, narrow windows are topped with slight pediments, and the porch roof has underside dentils and highly decorative spindlework over square posts.

SLEVIN HOUSE AT 417 EAST FRONT (BUILT C. 1866). This house was built by Rosana Slevin, probably the wife of Patrick S. Slevin, a well-known attorney and Civil War officer. It has been called "the vernacular answer to some of the 'high style' Queen Anne homes in the area." Note the front-facing intersecting gables with a small semi-circular window in the front and the other windows of varying size and shape. Extensive renovation has been made over the years. It was once owned by St. Rose Catholic Church and used as a rectory.

HOUSTON BUILDING AT 200 LOUISIANA (BUILT C. 1867). Louisiana and Second has always been a key business site. Henry H. Houston bought this corner on which at least one earlier frame building once stood. The front is original, with a recessed entrance flanked by iron Doric columns. Two second-floor casement balconies with decorative ironwork replaced doors to two apartments entered from outdoor stairways. Those doors were then shortened to make windows. The building was later covered in stucco to protect its soft brick. (Courtesy of Lee Gagle.)

EBERLY BUILDING AT 201 LOUISIANA (BUILT IN 1867). This Renaissance Italianate building was built for shoemaker John Eberly and used for his shoe business for nearly 60 years. Noticeable features are the arcaded corbeled cornice in the front and three interior chimneys projecting from the sloping roof. Eberly, born in Germany, came here in 1848 and was presumably working at his trade when he built this building back when footwear was often custom-made on site.

MCKNIGHT HOUSE AT 227 WEST SECOND (BUILT C. 1868). This house, built by John McKnight, is described as Catalog Italianate with Gothic influence. Extensive remodeling by the Glen Charles family in the 1930s blurs its likely original look. A single window is set above a multi-paned bay. Incised woodwork decorates the peak of the gable. A pediment tops the front entry framed by pilasters and sidelights. McKnight was born here in 1827 and during the 1850s operated a grocery store on Louisiana.

SECOND ZOAR LUTHERAN CHURCH AT 314 EAST INDIANA (BUILT IN LATE 1860S). This was Zoar Lutheran Church's second church building, erected originally for a German singing group called the Perrysburg Saengerbund. The tower and steeple were added in 1895. In about 1916, the congregation built the original part of its present brick church on this site, and this building was moved across town, cut in half, and made into two small side-by-side houses at Mulberry and Indiana.

The owner of these two houses (once our Lutheran church) has just had them rejoined into a single dwelling at 329 Mulberry Street.

Six

1870–1880

Embers from a disastrous fire that burned down or damaged many downtown-area buildings also caused destruction of the old county courthouse. Townspeople immediately raised money and built a new one, offering it free of charge as a lure to regain the county seat. A second vote on the removal issue (the first was in 1866) still favored Bowling Green, and so after 40 years, it was confirmed that this town no longer had claim as the Wood County seat. During the controversy, the editors of Perrysburg and Bowling Green's newspapers amused the public and inflamed passions by conducting a colorful and vitriolic war of words.

The Cora Lock, the side-wheeler pictured here, was hauling passengers and barrels of fish to and from Toledo at this time. It was built for local businessman Levi Lock and named for his popular daughter. As a result of the big fire mentioned earlier, the town's first steam fire engine, the Mohawk, was ordered.

During this decade, drainage of the Great Black Swamp was well under way. It became one of the most notable water control achievements known in this country. Before long, there were to be 25,000 miles of ditches diverting water into Lake Erie. At the same time, clearing the surrounding virgin forests for agricultural use fed a growing woodworking industry. Barrel staves, railroad ties, fruit boxes, windows sashes, siding, and flooring were produced here. At the same time, local workers were turning out such diverse products as barrel hoops, bed springs, and carriages.

At the beginning of this period, John D. Rockefeller and his brother William created the Standard Oil Company in Cleveland and were about to take advantage of the discovery of oil and natural gas in Wood County. Meanwhile, women of Perrysburg organized the Aid Society for the relief of sufferers of the disastrous fire that destroyed much of Chicago and the terrible forest fires that struck almost simultaneously and took over a thousand lives in Michigan and Wisconsin. Also here in town, the temperance movement saw church women smash saloon windows.

LOCK HOUSE AT 208 EAST FRONT (BUILT C. 1870). Levi C. Lock built this Tuscan Villa Italianate house, one of the most authentic examples of this style in the immediate area. It has a flat, hipped roof with a broad overhang embellished by paired eaves brackets, and round-headed windows with corbeled brick drip moldings. The round-headed double-door front entrance has stained glass panes under a fanlight. A porch originally extended across the front. Lock was a business partner of Dr. E. D. Peck and was the owner of the popular side-wheeler steamer *Cora Lock*.

COOK-FINKBEINER HOUSE AT 308 EAST FRONT (BUILT C. 1870). This house with Italianate details may have been built by Asher Cook (see page 69), who owned several lots in this neighborhood. Christopher Finkbeiner, a German immigrant who came here in 1847, was an early occupant. Single brackets support the low-pitched roof with wide overhanging eaves, and the second-floor windows have molded pediments. Double Doric columns support the porch with its diamond-patterned windows. Finkbeiner, former mayor, postmaster, township clerk, and county recorder, was a local businessman who lost a leg serving in the Civil War.

HAMILTON HOUSE AT 308 WEST FRONT (BUILT IN 1870S). Born in Connecticut, Dr. Horatio Arnold Hamilton came here in 1854 to join his uncle, Dr. Erasmus D. Peck, upon the death of Peck's partner in the cholera epidemic. He built this fine frame Greek Revival/Italianate house with the eaves brackets, raked cornice with entablature, wood finials atop the window pediments, and the slender column porch supports with scrolled brackets. Matching pilasters frame the door containing original etched glass. The narrow downstairs front windows are nearly floor to ceiling high.

VAN SOYSE HOUSE AT 320 WEST FRONT (BUILT C. 1870). The builder of this Colonial Revival house is not definitely known, but it has been associated with James Van Soyse. It has a hipped roof with a large overhang and dormers on the front, left, and right sides. The front door is topped by a triangular pediment with dentils and flanked by fluted Doric pilasters.

ROSS HOUSE AT 128 EAST FRONT (BUILT C. 1870). Pennsylvanian James W. Ross came here in 1834 and built this Italian Villa-style house. It is distinguished by its square cupola, or tower, which is rare in this area. Notice the pediments on all four sides of the tower over the Palladian windows. Abundant decorative details include tall and narrow windows under incised stone lentils, and finials and pendants in the gable peaks. Ross was, among other things, an educator who founded a private school and later a school examiner, county coroner, and township clerk.

It is typical in small towns that one of the nicest houses often ends up as a funeral home. With additions such as the drive-through porch and rear add-ons, this one in 1930 became and served for two generations and more as the Witzler Funeral Home.

THORNTON HOUSE AT 426 WEST FRONT (BUILT C. 1870). This house is associated with the John H. Thornton family, operators of a brick factory that supplied brick for many of the early commercial and residential structures in the area. It has a dominant front gable with a carved vergeboard under which the ground floor windows are tall and narrow. Two almost side-by-side doors may indicate that the left wing is an addition—though one door could have been a so-called funeral door to accommodate a casket. Thornton joined his father, who could have been the builder of this house, in the brick business and in time headed it.

OLD EXCHANGE BANK AT 110 LOUISIANA (BUILT IN 1871). This small building, or an earlier version of it, is claimed to be Wood County's oldest bank site. The present building originally had two prominent semi-circular brick corbeled arches in the center facade, with attractive masonry ornamentation. There was a simple double door entrance flush with the facade, with a large window just to the right. Dr. Erasmus D. Peck (see page 50) was the principal organizer of this bank that was liquidated after eight years.

OLD MASONIC BUILDING AT 103–105 LOUISIANA (BUILT C. 1872). Behind the contemporary facade are one or more much older buildings. An 1869 newspaper article refers to the possible addition of an upper story to one of them, and the erection of a Masonic hall. There is a later newspaper reference to "the old Masonic lodge designed by Langdon and Hohley of Toledo and built by Leon LaFarree in 1920."

LADD HOUSE AT 239 EAST FRONT (BUILT IN 1872). This small house is said to have been built by Judge David Ladd for his daughter Anna. It is similar in style to country cottages made popular by architect A. J. Downing in the first half of the 1800s. It features narrow, plain vergeboards with a carved gable ornament and a mansard canopy over a single front window. Ladd was an associate judge of Common Pleas Court and a U.S. land agent. The tombstone of one of his three wives, discovered in the back yard, is now set in concrete in the patio. Her remains are believed to be elsewhere.

F. R. MILLER HOUSE AT 241 EAST FRONT (BUILT C. 1872). A classic Italianate structure built by a German-born merchant who came here in 1850, this home has the typical roof cresting and incised stone lintels over tall, narrow windows. Single brackets are beneath the wide roof overhang that is decorated with dentils. The double front door has arched panes with a floral etched transom. The original carriage house in the rear has matching patterns. Miller was a lieutenant colonel and commandant of Fort McHenry in Baltimore during the Civil War. He was also a mayor of Perrysburg.

ELABORATE FRONT PORTICO. The unique feature of this home is the elaborate front portico—all covered in stamped tin. The ornamental columns have thick composite capitals, topped by a balustrade.

TOWN HALL AT WALNUT AND INDIANA (BUILT IN 1872, RAZED IN 1963). This classic Victorian building designed by Toledo architects Rumbaugh and Fallis was the product of the fierce rivalry between Perrysburg and Bowling Green to be the county seat. After fire destroyed the abandoned courthouse here in 1872, and while the results of an earlier election on the move were being challenged, citizens quickly raised money to build and offer this building free of charge. It was 101 feet long, 69 feet wide, and had a slate mansard roof and a 64.5-foot tower. A second county vote, whose procedures were also questionable, still favored Bowling Green, so township offices were moved into the ground floor, and the name became Township Hall and later, Town Hall. A second-floor auditorium was used by the community for many years.

LATER TOWN HALL. Town Hall looked like this when it was razed in 1963 after the second-story ceiling and rafters collapsed the morning of the day teenagers were to have had a dance. It was owned at that time by the city and deemed too frail and costly to restore.

COOK HOUSE AT 409 EAST FRONT (BUILT IN 1873). This is a pretentious Italianate house worthy of the prominence of its builder, Asher Cook—lawyer, judge, former mayor, state representative, and state and national politician. The architecture features include typical tall and narrow windows with decorative wooden headers, wide overhanging eaves over massive single brackets, frieze windows, double front doors with panes, bays on either side, and a brick carriage house with cupola in the rear. Cook helped revise the Ohio constitution and was known as one of the best constitutional lawyers in the state. He took a leading role in organizing the Republican Party.

ASHER COOK'S ORIGINAL CARRIAGE HOUSE. Cook came from Pennsylvania. Despite lacking a formal education, he became an attorney and on his own learned to read and speak French, German, Spanish, and Latin, leaving a sizeable collection of such books.

HENRY E. AVERILL HOUSE AT 333 EAST FRONT (BUILT IN 1873). A Hudson River Mode Gothic Revival, this house was designed by Isaac Hobbs & Son of New York. It was the wedding gift of Henry P. Averill (see page 29) to his son. Curvilinear vergeboards in the gables, ornamental porch scrollwork, and the double door with transom are typical of this style. The house had all the latest conveniences including the town's first indoor water closets, gas lighting, and speaking tubes. It remained in the Averill family until 1957. Henry E. was a Civil War veteran, an attorney, and an assistant to the Ohio Attorney General, and he later served in the office of Adjutant General. He was also in railroad construction and was an auditor for the Ohio & Mississippi Railroad and the Standard Oil Company when it was in Cleveland. (*left*) The house features round and arched windows and this double window covered with a decorative canopy.

DOUGLAS HOUSE AT 340 WEST FRONT (BUILT IN 1874). This Italianate-style brick house was built by Joseph Lindsay as a wedding present to his granddaughter, Mrs. James L. Douglas. Her father, Daniel Lindsay, lived next door (see page 17). It has a hipped roof and a variety of multi-paned windows, most with segmental arches. The original front porch was removed and the lower front window replaced with a picture window. The front door is flanked by fluted Doric pilasters topped with a broken pediment with a centerpiece urn. The rear of the house has been enlarged, with the first floor walls of brick and the second of wood. Little is known of the Douglas family, who later left Perrysburg.

FITZGERALD HOUSE AT 323 WEST SECOND (BUILT C. 1875). The most visible Gothic Revival feature on this modest house is the steep front gable with the decorative vergeboards. Unusual small three-pane ribbon windows just above the porch roof and the right side of the house are sources of light low on the second floor. This was Irish-born Michael Fitzgerald's house. He operated a grocery and saloon on Louisiana.

POWELL-DENISON HOUSE AT 304 WEST FRONT (BUILT IN 1870S). This house is often associated with Charles F. Chapman, who acquired it shortly after opening an office here for his national woodenware business. It has an interesting combination of Greek Revival and Queen Anne details, the most striking being the ornate scrollwork on the two porches. The asymmetrical variety of windows, including the one in the front attic with quarter-circle panes, are typical of the Queen Anne style.

This is an undated photograph of this house before the porch on the left side was extended. There is also now a two-story addition in the rear.

TYLER-ROETHER BUILDING AT 111 EAST SECOND (BUILT C. 1875). This building is a typical small-town lawyer or doctor's office building, of which it was both. It was built by Michael Roether, a German-born cabinet maker, for attorney James R. Tyler. In 1896, Roether's son, Henry R. Roether, bought it for his medical practice. Tyler was one of the most capable criminal lawyers in the state. He served as mayor twice. Roether, a Perrysburg native, practiced here for 41 years and was also once mayor. This building has been in the Roether family for 109 years.

WIELAND HOUSE AT 976 LOUISIANA (BUILT C. 1875). This house was possibly built by Fred Hillabrand, who in 1887 sold it to John M. Wieland. Attractive scrolled brackets and turned posts and balusters on the porch are worth noting. Single narrow six-over-six windows are in the gables, which have Queen Anne-style fishscale siding. It is assumed that the Wieland mentioned here was one of two brothers who operated a tannery at the river's edge at the end of Mulberry Street, or a descendant of one of them.

LaFarree House at 523 West Second (Built in 1870s). The front of this house looked like this 95 years ago. It sat for about 125 years at 89 Linden Lane, which was named Commercial Street originally, in one of the oldest parts of town. In 1997, it was moved to its present location to make way for a St. Rose Church parking lot. George LaFarree, a carpenter by trade, built the house, whose main feature was the delicate scrollwork on the porch posts. They are like flower stems arching out toward the top. Mrs. LaFarree is sitting between her two daughters, Frances and Norine. A third daughter, Irene, is said to be taking the picture.

The House Today. The original front porch was screened and made into a wrap-around on the left side. Other additions were made, especially in the rear.

HANSON HOUSE AT 203 EAST SECOND (BUILT C. 1876). This is another brick Italianate house, built by Nathaniel L. Hanson, who came here in 1871 from New Hampshire to be a teller of a short-lived bank. He later organized and managed the Citizens Banking Company. The tall windows feature incised stone lintels. Paired brackets support the eaves over a broad cornice beneath which is a dentil pattern. The double-door entrance is topped by a transom of etched glass, and there are bay windows on the left and right sides of the house.

LUCAS BUILDING AT 219 LOUISIANA (BUILT IN LATE 1800S). This French Second Empire-style building started as a home and grocery believed built by Henry Lucas. Under the name Broske's, it continues as a favorite breakfast and conversation hangout for merchants and politicians. SWAT members perched on the distinctive mansard roof to guard Pres. Ronald Reagan during a campaign speech from the rear of a nearby train. The roof has a large overhang decorated with dentils and ornamental brackets. The windows have stone knobbed lentils.

CENTENNIAL BLOCK AT 102–104 LOUISIANA (BUILT IN 1876). Built by merchant Frederick R. Miller (see page 67) and designed by well-known Toledo architect E. O. Fallis, this building unites two stores divided from basement to roof by a wall in which hot-air furnace flues and ventilators serve both sides. The ceiling is covered in stamped tin. The upper facade is accented by corbeled brickwork and eaves brackets. The upstairs left side contained an auditorium seating about 250, the scene of many public events. The store space on the right was known as "Drug Store Corner." (*below*) Cast iron Corinthian columns at ground level entrance help support the super structure.

Seven
1880–1890

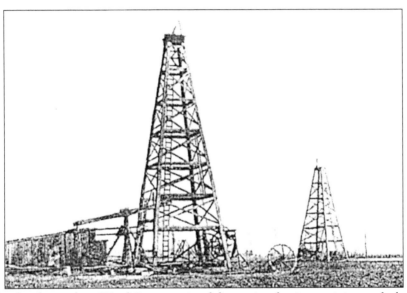

During this decade, southern Wood County enjoyed discovering that it was sitting on the largest then-known oil and gas resource in the country, but to the disappointment of Perrysburg taxpayers, drilling to considerable depth proved our town to be on the outside edge of the bonanza. Nevertheless, at least one natural gas line was laid through town, and the Exchange Hotel became the first customer.

There were still fewer than 2,000 people in Perrysburg, and it was becoming a Toledo suburban residential town, but still a market center for area farmers. Because of lumber demand, woodworking was still flourishing, with wagon-loads of logs being hauled in by horse and oxen and rolled down the river embankment on West Front Street. They were then rafted to Toledo.

The town's arguably finest business structure, the Centennial Block, was erected on "Drug Store Corner" at Front and Louisiana, and attorney D. K. Hollenbeck had the first telephone. It ran about three blocks between his office and home. Someone counted the residences of 26 business and professional men in the first several blocks of East and West Second Streets and suggested that it be called "Business Men's Row." The town's three-story Union School burned down, but plans were made immediately for a new one, which was built and in operation by the following fall. The Presbyterian Church, then located on the site of today's Way Library, was also destroyed by fire. A crowd of thousands helped St. Rose de Lima Catholic Church celebrate the laying of the cornerstone for its handsome new Gothic building.

Gen. James A. Garfield was elected president in 1880, but six months later Gen. Chester A. Arthur succeeded him when Garfield died of an assassin's bullets. By the end of the decade, William Henry Harrison's grandson, Benjamin, was president. Here in Perrysburg, our mayors in succession were Dr. John H. Rheinfrank, James H. Pierce, Fred Yeager, and Dr. Isaac Bowers, all of whom were owners of properties mentioned in this book.

AMMON BUILDING AT 117 LOUISIANA (BUILT C. 1880). It is not certain whether this narrow three-story commercial building was constructed by John Ammon in 1877, or by Rudolph Danz in 1888 and sold later to John Ammon Jr., but it is associated with the Ammon family. The front upper windows are six-over-six with carved arched keystone lentils. There is a brick cornice with dentils and a stepped roofline. Among occupants over the years have been a hardware store, dairy company, clothing store, and the present day travel agency. (*below*) The front of building has carved arched keystone lentils and a fancy brick corbeled cornice with a dentil effect.

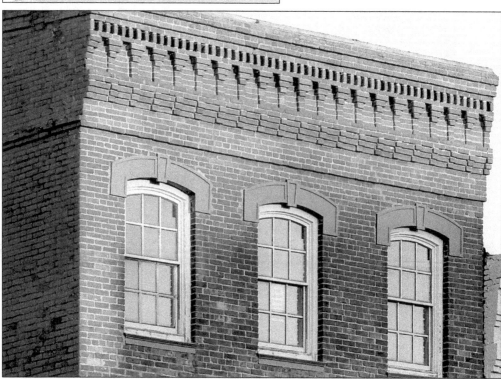

PIERCE HOUSE AT 146 WEST FRONT (BUILT C. 1885). A large variety of classical windows, mullions, and moldings are seen in this house of James H. Pierce. Few exterior alterations are evident. It is of Queen Anne style, with an attractive full porch covered by a roof with balustrade, double front doors with etched panes, and a wooden water table around the entire building. Pierce came here from New York state in 1857. Over the years, he was a merchant, lumberman, once owner of the next door Exchange Hotel, and two-term mayor. He was also a county commissioner and township trustee. (*below*) This is a good view of the variety of window shapes and sizes in the house.

SEILING HOUSE AT 904 SANDUSKY (BUILT C. 1885). Records are vague about who built this former farm house, but one owner attributes it to Christopher Seiling, who acquired the property in 1873 and built it for the Dr. Henry Roether family (see page 73). A rambling cross-gabled structure, it has porch posts containing decorative scrollwork, corbeled chimneys, a cut-stone foundation, and numerous windows. Now surrounded by houses, the farm was the site of the Loomis family's Homewood Dairy, which delivered milk by horse and wagon and was the first in town to pasteurize its bottled milk. It was bought by Babcock Dairy of Toledo in 1946. (*below*) Until quite recently, this large barn and silo behind the house still existed. Now well inside the city limits, the site was one of several outlying working farms in Perrysburg.

LOCK FAMILY HOUSE AT 220 EAST FRONT (PROBABLY BUILT C. 1885). Vernacular Victorian architecture with a touch of Queen Anne features, this house may have been built by the Levi Lock family after his death, or even moved from another location. Early descriptions mention a now removed vergeboard with five rosettes in the front gable. The picture window in downstairs front is likely a later addition. Note the interesting recessed corner front entrance with spindlework detailing.

This undated photograph shows an early fire fighting apparatus that was pulled through downtown Perrysburg and nearby streets and then connected to two existing cisterns filled with river water.

SIMMONS HOUSE AT 10302 FREMONT PIKE (BUILT IN 1887). Edwin H. Simmons built this farm house on the edge of town. His granddaughter, Mary Cranker, fought stubbornly but successfully to get it on the National Register for preservation purposes and to honor this area's early homesteading activities. The house is a balloon-frame vernacular structure with ornamental touches typical of the time. A distinctive feature is a funeral door on the left side of the porch to accommodate a casket. Simmons was a successful farmer, businessman, and township trustee. (*below*) Jigsawn corner brackets with scalloped edges and delicate incised pattern decorate the porch posts.

TOLMAN HOUSE AT 420 WALNUT (BUILT IN 1888). This modest Victorian house was built for Perrysburg industrialist Sewell P. Tolman, who came here from Keene, New Hampshire, to buy an interest in a wood box factory that he eventually owned. The boxes and crates Tolman made were largely for fruit. Noteworthy are the extremely narrow front windows and gingerbread ornamentation in the front gable and on the porch.

DODGE HOUSE AT 345 WEST FRONT (BUILT IN 1880S). There may have been a house on this site as early as the 1830s, but this version, enlarged in recent years, is attributed to Henry H. Dodge, a prominent attorney. Having Queen Anne details, the irregular roofline includes a triangular front pediment within a pediment over an off-center door with narrow glazing and sidelights. The back overhangs a steep slope to the river. Dodge came here from New York state in 1852 and was considered dean of the Wood County bar, serving for 10 years as judge of common pleas court.

HOOVER HOUSE AT 209 EAST SECOND (BUILT C. 1890). Horace M. Hoover is thought to have built this frame house with Queen Anne characteristics. It has a steeply pitched roof of irregular shape with a dominant front gable and bay windows. Most of the windows are very tall and narrow, and there is an interesting angled corner window in the right first floor. The main and side porches have classical columns instead of the more common turned posts.

MUNGER HOUSE AT 215 EAST SECOND (BUILT IN 1890). Another rambling but virtually unchanged Victorian home is this Queen Anne built by George Munger Sr. It remained in that prominent family through four generations. The paired column wrap-around porch features a dentiled cornice, balustrade, and latticework underneath. The front gable has an elliptical, or lunette, window. Munger, with a brother, established a butcher shop that for 50 years was a downtown landmark.

Eight
1890–1900

Two giant steps forward during this decade were the building of an electric generation plant at Third and Walnut, and the inauguration of electric streetcar service between Perrysburg and East Toledo. Eventually it extended to Maumee and Bowling Green. Civil War veteran William Witzler, former owner of a sawmill south of town, won the bid to build a generating plant to light 28 arc street lamps that were serviced from horseback (replacing carbon sticks).

On the northeast corner of Louisiana and Indiana, the landmark original brownstone Way Library was built, finally using money left for that purpose by attorney Willard V. Way nearly 20 years earlier. The same year, local architect Arthur Hitchcock of the Toledo firm of Bacon & Huber was hired to design a new school with an 80-foot tower that topped the horizon viewed from several miles away.

Just off Louisiana on West Front Street, Dr. John Rheinfrank and his physician son, William, converted a brick home and business place into Rheinfrank Hospital, which was to gain renown as a thyroid treatment center. Wheel manufacturing saw its beginning here during this period.

There were other noticeable physical changes in Perrysburg during this last decade of the 19th century. A fire destroyed six business places in the 200 block of Louisiana, and the local editor decried the vulnerability of downtown frame buildings. Henceforth, brick replacements became the general trend in town.

Still living here was John (Alf) Wilson, who enlisted in the Civil War at Perrysburg and who was the fireman on the train of the famous Mitchell Raiders. This group daringly stole the train from the Confederates, but when caught, Wilson escaped execution. William Jennings Bryan, presidential candidate, spoke to our citizens from the back of a train. Nationally, Perrysburg weathered the depression of 1893 and the short Spanish-American War.

HARRY BARTON HOUSE AT 424 EAST FRONT (BUILT IN 1898). Harry C. Barton had Toledo architects Baker and Hitchcock, the latter a Perrysburg resident, design this house with recognizable Queen Anne and Shingle elements. Notice the steeply pitched roof of irregular shape, asymmetrical facade, exposed rafters where the roof protrudes, patterned shingles, and other devices used to avoid a smooth-walled appearance. Barton was the son of well-known English-born merchant William Barton and spent most of his adult life in Toledo.

HOFFMAN HOUSE AT 221 EAST SECOND (BUILT C. 1898). Designed by Perrysburg architect George Rheinfrank Sr., this basically Queen Anne-style house built by Christopher A. Hoffman (see page 47) features a three-sided two-story bay topped by a conical roof, giving it the resemblance of a tower. The lower story walls of the house are of clapboard and the upper are in shingle. The flared porch roof is supported by Ionic columns. Hoffman began in the grocery and saloon business, a common combination at the time. He also operated a restaurant.

PRESBYTERIAN CHURCH AT 200 EAST SECOND (BUILT IN 1892). A blend of Stick and Gothic Revival is the style of this building. Stick style, rare in this area, stresses the wall surface as a decorative element, with application of vertical, horizontal, and diagonal trim, plus decorative trusses in the gables. Architect Charles Sturgis designed this church to replace one burned in 1875. The attractive bell tower features pointed lancet windows in each face. Other than loss of visible details covered by artificial siding, church officials have done a good job of preserving this fine old structure. Major additions have been made to the rear. (*below*) This photograph, probably taken in the early or mid-1900s, shows the Stick decorative trim on the exterior walls of the building.

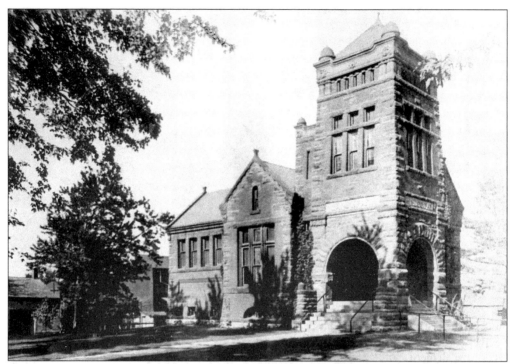

WAY LIBRARY AT 101 EAST INDIANA (BUILT IN 1892 AND NOW RAZED). Beginning with an endowment of nearly $30,000 for books and a building from the estate of Willard Vibard Way (see page 19), this Richardsonian Romanesque building designed by Toledo architects Bacon & Huber was the first library in Wood County. The massive stone-wall style was of red brick and brown blocks that were hand cut and dressed on site. Interior floors were wooden, and a winding staircase led to the director's office in the tower. Despite a lively campaign to preserve it, the building was determined "too small, too leaky, too drafty, too clammy, and too ugly" to save and was torn down in 1958.

A Neo-Colonial Revival building replaced the one above in 1950, and in 2001, it was doubled in size with this attractive matching version, primarily by keeping the original exterior walls intact and adding 50,000 square feet around them—plus changing the entrance to the north side where land was cleared for a large parking area. Munger, Munger + Associates were the architects for both buildings. (Courtesy of Wurzell Photography and Video.)

ST. ROSE CATHOLIC CHURCH AT 215 EAST FRONT (BUILT IN 1893). Work began on this fine old Gothic Revival church, claimed by some to be the first stone church in the Maumee Valley, in 1889. It was designed by John Burkart of Kenton, Ohio, and built of Sandusky bluestone lined on the interior with some 400,000 bricks hauled from East Toledo. It features buttressed walls capped by pinnacles or turrets, pointed arch windows with decorative tracery, and imported leaded stained glass. Two small entrances flank the main, each with double wooden doors set within Berea sandstone arches. Midway up the square tower under the steeple is a niche containing a large statue of patron St. Rose of Lima. Despite a congregation of only about 150 families at the time, the indebtedness for the building was paid in only 11 years. (*below*) Exterior features in high-style Gothic architecture tend to come to a sharp point, both in houses and especially in cathedral-like churches.

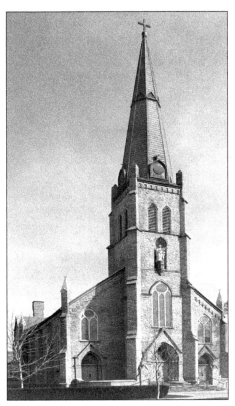

SARGENT HOUSE AT 232 WEST FRONT (BUILT C. 1894). This house was built by Henry H. Sargent. Aside from its shingle wall cladding, identifying features in this variable style include the cross gable gambrel roof and multi-level eaves. A pent, or short extension roof, extends above the front bay and below it across the entire front is another pent roof. On the right side, a gable over a sunroom drops midway down the roof, supported by two Ionic columns. Sargent came here in 1893, having purchased a partnership in the renamed Chapman-Sargent Woodenware Company.

MADDY HOUSE AT 508 WEST FRONT (BUILT C. 1895). John C. Maddy tore down a house on this site to build this 12-room Queen Anne. The distinctive porch with balustrade has Doric columns, and the main entrance is on the left corner under a pediment with decorative molding. Tiny brackets are beneath all the eaves. There is a steeply pitched irregular shaped roof, gables, and numerous windows—55 in number. Maddy was a successful Toledo grain dealer and elevator manager.

RHEINFRANK HOUSE AT 228 EAST FRONT (BUILT IN 1895). Dr. John H. Rheinfrank came here from Michigan at the end of the Civil War to practice medicine for nearly 60 years. Bacon & Huber of Toledo designed his Queen Anne house with the large wrap-around porch with slender Doric columns, double front doors, and the Palladian window-shaped opening in the front gable. Wall siding is clapboard on the first floor, and shingle on the second. A now altered carriage house and well pump house still exist on the property. Dr. Rheinfrank was once the mayor, and he established Rheinfrank Hospital (see page 54).

WELL PUMP HOUSE. Even the well pump house follows the Queen Anne style for exterior wall cladding.

COMSTOCK HOUSE AT 401 WEST FRONT (BUILT IN 1895). Here is another example of Shingle architecture built by Plain Township native William Comstock. This adaptation of other architectural traditions features an irregular roofline, a tower, gables, turrets, and prominent bay windows typical of the Queen Anne style from which the Shingle style derived. Between the two ends of the house and on the right side are ogee-arched dormers. Comstock taught school, farmed, owned a drug store, and became a successful traveling salesman, selling caskets. (*left*) In the upper left corner of this house is a good example of an oriel window in a recessed arch of the gable over a set of multi-paned windows braced by Ionic pilasters.

Nine
1900–1910

For over 50 years, Perrysburg's population held steady at just under 2,000. It was now beginning to grow. Trolley transportation (the car above is in front of the H. E. Averill house; see page 70) and the first automobiles were luring new residents. A 10-mile-an-hour speed limit was being enforced in town. On East River Road, Toledo industrialists Henry L. Thompson, George R. Ford, and W. W. Knight bought some 2,000 feet of land fronting the river to establish their summer residences, and later permanent mansions, the first of 13 that would eventually be built along this road between Perrysburg and Rossford.

Use of private water wells slowed early in this decade when a municipal system drawing water from deep wells in the river flats was approved. The Soldiers and Sailors Monument, a long-sought memorial to Civil War and later Spanish-American War servicemen was finally made possible by privately raised funds and the donation of a site on "Corn Cob Hill," now Hood Park. Up at Fort Meigs battleground, by now owned by the state but still considered a Perrysburg park by residents, hundreds helped dedicate an 82-foot-tall granite obelisk erected in memory of the Ohio, Kentucky, Pennsylvania, and Virginia soldiers who died there during the British and Indian sieges in 1813.

On Louisiana, motion pictures were introduced in a nickelodeon, and around the corner from Louisiana the venerable Exchange Hotel suffered a fire that finally put it out of business after almost 85 years.

Meanwhile, people just outside Perrysburg were still sending their small children to a dozen or so one-room schoolhouses in the township. As electricity was not available outside of town to power saws and hoists, neighbors gathered on "barn-raising day" to prepare timber and put up barns and large outbuildings. In town, the Schlect Ford Agency on Louisiana Avenue sold its first car, probably the new model priced at under $900, and residents no doubt rejoiced with others of the nation's consumers over availability of the new safety razor, and electric iron, toaster, and washing machines.

SCHLECT BUILDING AT 209 LOUISIANA (BUILT PROBABLY C. 1900). Two destructive fires in 1891 and 1900 cloud the records as to who exactly was responsible for replacement with this Commercial Colonial Revival brick building. We pick up its history when William Schlect was using the right side of it, first for his father's earlier harness, collars, whips, farm implements, wagons, and buggies business, and still later, as the agency for Ford cars, beginning with the Model T. William Schlect was born and raised in Perrysburg. His son, Gus, continued the business.

TOWN'S FIRST CAR AGENCY. The first car sold was shipped here by freight train and assembled. And that sale of one car constituted the total sales for that year.

FORMER CONVALESCENT HOME AT 341 WEST FRONT (BUILT PROBABLY IN 1900S). Who built this house and when is unknown, but its interesting facade details are worthy of being shown here. The first floor is of painted brick and the upper level is board and batten. The downstairs windows are topped with elliptical fanlights that match the arched door, which appears to be an addition. It has long been a private residence, but in 1937, it was being advertised as "Riverview Convalesant [sic] Home, A Private Modern Institution For Invalids, Aged and Incurable Cases."

FINKBEINER HOUSE AT 305 WEST SECOND (BUILT PROBABLY c. 1900). Another structure of unknown age and original ownership, this Colonial Revival-style house was in the William A. Finkbeiner family for more than 90 years. The family is believed responsible for most of its current appearance. Perrysburg-born Finkbeiner was in the mercantile business here and in East Toledo.

MOSER BUILDING AT 111 LOUISIANA (BUILT IN 1900). Called a commercial Colonial, this 22-foot-wide, 3-story building was designed by George Rheinfrank Sr. for George W. Moser. The roof is stepped, and there is a projecting eave with scrolled mullions running across the top and a frieze with dentils. Moser, born near Waterville, once owned the Christopher Hoffman Grocery and Restaurant building (see page 47) then next door before it burned down.

DANZ HOUSE AT 248 EAST FRONT (BUILT C. 1910). Swiss immigrant Rudolph Danz built this gambrel-roofed Colonial Revival house (this subtype was also known as Dutch Colonial). Foot-wide segments of roof on the left and right ends of the cornice extend from the peaks. A portico is supported by Doric columns with a single door flanked by pilasters and sidelights. The left portion of the house was extended in later years. Danz came to Perrysburg in 1871 and was the town baker for 29 years.

"Syndicate" Building at 112 Louisiana (Built in 1903). This commercial Italianate building was built by a group of local men who got together at the turn of the 20th century to invest in property in the first block of our main street—hence its identifying name. The facade of the small building is architecturally interesting in that it contains the same size bricks for all features, with no stone or concrete embellishments. The arrangement of T-shaped corbeled brickwork between saw-tooth belts over four small circular window openings is especially interesting. While not publicly identified, evidence suggests that Jacob Davis, long-time owner of Davis Hardware in this block was one of the investors. He came to Perrysburg from Buffalo, New York, in 1879, served in the Union navy before that during the Civil War, and was a village councilman, school board member, and president of the Citizens Banking Company.

HOOD PARK SOLDIERS AND SAILORS MONUMENT AT LOUISIANA AND FRONT (UNVEILED IN 1902). For many years there was a clamor for a monument to Civil War servicemen. By the time this one was built, it included those of the Spanish-American War. After voters refused to tax themselves to pay for it, private donations were enough to have Eckhardt Monument of Toledo produce this Vermont granite figure located just west of the Perry statue.

HOOD PARK AT THE TURN OF THE 20TH CENTURY. The site for this park was donated by John Hood, who almost realized his desire for anonymity in that for many years it was known as Monument Park.

HOLLENBECK BUILDING AT 106 LOUISIANA (BUILT IN 1903). This commercial building was built as an investment by Daniel K. Hollenbeck who practiced law here for some 60 years and was once our mayor. The most noticeable features are the small windows in the upper front. The cornice across the top story features dentils, and there are supporting iron columns in the interior. The first occupant was the J. Davis Hardware Store. A second front entrance is an addition. (*below*) This set of eye-like windows are surrounded by an egg and dart motif, which is also carried out on the first story pilasters.

PERRYSBURG BANK BUILDING AT 131 LOUISIANA (BUILT IN 1905). This is a familiar downtown landmark designed by George B. Rheinfrank Sr. for the Perrysburg Banking Co. Built of cast sand blocks, it originally was a long, narrow two-story building with office rental space on the second floor. The first major alteration was the bricking over of the lower half of the facade and changing of the entrance, which had featured a plate glass window topped by ornamental prism glass. Unpopular with some citizens, this was soon replaced with the present white wooden fascia, and the drive-through portico was added. Incorporated in 1906, the bank merged with the Bank of Wood County and later became a part of Huntington National Bank. (*below*) Pictured here is an architect's sketch of the original bank building.

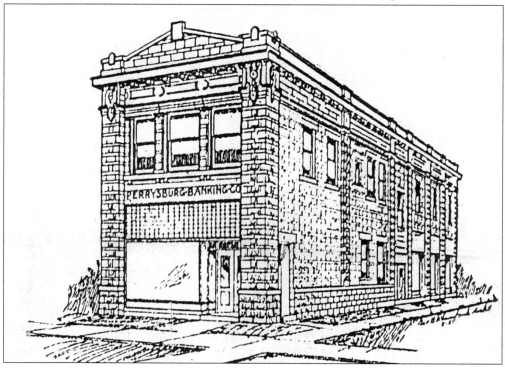

VEITCH HOUSE AT 420 EAST FRONT (BUILT IN 1906). Two-term mayor and long-time merchant William J. Veitch built this pattern-book Queen Anne house. A turret-like dormer faces the front, and an indented frieze with dentil-like blocks is in the left gable, with decorative brackets in the right one. First floor walls are of clapboard and the second of shingles. After a time in a Toledo wholesale grocery firm, Veitch bought the William Barton dry goods store, which he operated for more than 40 years while contributing as a civic leader.

FRALIC BUILDING AT 203 LOUISIANA (BUILT IN 1906). Who built whatever might have sat earlier at this site is unknown, but Richard Fralic built today's version. Interesting details include gold-painted rosettes on the frieze beneath the cornice, and beneath that a pair of corbeled panels. The upper front windows have stone trim with keystones over them, and a stone block in the upper center is engraved with "R. Fralic, 1906." Fralic, born in Canada, used the building for his grocery. It now houses a pub and restaurant.

NEIDERHOUSE HOUSE AT EAST SOUTH BOUNDARY AND ELM (BUILT IN 1908). Here is an example of a house remodeled and totally unrecognizable as the original. This photograph is of the original house that sat on this site and was built by Charles F. Neiderhouse as the seat of his 60-acre farm; all of it is now well inside the city limits, but it then sat at the edge of cornfields along with the barn and silo just across South Boundary. The two-story house had a steep gambrel roof, a full front porch, and gabled upstairs dormers. (*below*) In 1958, architect Robert Lutz designed this renovation with its regular pitched roof over wide frieze boards and a long one-story wing on the right.

Ten

1910–1930

These two combined decades span the final architectural period covered in this book.

Perrysburg celebrated its 100th birthday and experienced World War I during these years. Today's versions (not including very recent additions) of Zoar Lutheran and First United Methodist Churches were built, along with what was to be a long lasting sixth bridge across the same shallows of the river. Louisiana Avenue and Second Street were paved with brick, the former with trolley tracks running down the middle. Speaking of which, public bus transportation brought an end to trolleys here toward the end of this period, and the tracks were covered over and traffic signals installed at busy corners to control auto traffic.

Our only public school building was enlarged in the rear to better accommodate the high school that existed there until 1930 when the first new high school was built at Indiana and Elm Streets. St. Rose Catholic parish also built its elementary school at about this time. Out at West Sixth and Mulberry, a modern factory building went up to house the manufacture of a new product, steel wool.

Along East River Road between here and Rossford, a row of baronial estates built during this period (replacing mostly large, rambling summer cottages) has been called by one preservationist "irreplaceable monuments to an era of great wealth attained by a number of Toledo's industrial leaders." And in town, the Palace Theater began offering motion pictures and live entertainment.

By this time in Perrysburg's history, over a dozen styles of recognizable architecture, to one degree or another, were represented in the immediate area: Greek Revival, Gothic Revival, Italianate, Second Empire, Queen Anne, Shingle, Richardsonian Romanesque, Folk Victorian, Colonial Revival, Tudor, Spanish Mission, Prairie, and Craftsman—a remarkable collection for a town of under 5,000 people.

FRANK THORNTON HOUSE AT 220 WEST INDIANA (BUILT IN 1913). Representing a bit of Americana, here is a Sears and Roebuck kit house, one of as many as 22 models once offered in their catalog. Ready-cut houses like this, ranging from $600 to several thousand, were shipped by rail with assembly instructions. This one was for the family of Frank Thornton, our town marshal, who had earlier been shot to death while arresting criminals. It replaced their house that had been badly damaged in a fire on this site.

SPILKER HOUSE AT 145 WEST SECOND (BUILT C. 1914). This house sits on the site of a former carriage, wagon, and blacksmith manufactory, and it is believed the house was built by Edward J. Spilker. Normally of simple symmetrical shape, this version of American Foursquare architecture has seen a number of additions, especially in the rear where there are some intriguing gable arrangements. The three tapered Bungalow-style porch supports and a variety of irregularly placed windows are interesting.

OLD MUNICIPAL BUILDING AT 111–113 WEST SECOND (BUILT C. 1914). Although created in 1816, Perrysburg didn't have a city hall much more elaborate than a series of fire apparatus shelters with some office space, until the town bought the site for this building, the facade of which is believed to cover at least one earlier building. In 1914, it became the fire and police stations. Upstairs were the mayor's courtroom, the jail, and offices for several village officials.

NEW MUNICIPAL BUILDING. This new Municipal Building was built in the 1960s on the site of the old Town Hall (see page 68). Immediately to the right is the new Police Department building completed in 2004, and adjoining it is the new Municipal Court building.

H. L. Thompson House at 29953 Sussex Road (Built in 1915). This was the first of the large East River Road manors built along the river. It was built by Perrysburg native Henry L. Thompson Sr., who was one of Toledo's most influential and respected businessmen. Designed by Cleveland architects Walker and Weeks (and changed very little since), it sat on 25 acres of a self-supporting farm, complete with well-manicured orchards and plant and flower gardens, a huge greenhouse, a dairy herd, chickens, and horses. An attractive brick barn and caretaker's cottage are now converted residences, and most of the acreage is now part of The Hamlet development. The house is a blend of Tudor, Norman, Georgian, and Jacobethan architecture, and it features multiple front gables, a slate roof, large elaborate chimneys, and sections of half-timbered walls. Thompson went to work at an early age as an office boy for Bostwick-Braun, the wholesale hardware firm. By 1907, he was its president, and he also headed a large similar operation in Cleveland. He was a founder and president of a bank that became Toledo Trust under his leadership, and a director of a number of large Toledo companies.

SECOND LADD HOUSE AT 415 EAST SECOND (BUILT C. 1915). This rather modern looking house likely started as a three-room log cabin built as early as the 1830s, judging from hand-hewn understructure timbers. Judge David Ladd (see page 66) owned the property then, and he sold it two years later for much more than he paid for it. Scotland-born Robert Pargillis could have been the owner who made the first changes in it (including the addition of a second story while he was the owner in 1915). The house was also once the home of Charles E. Thompson, who started a company that designed most of the electric signs in Toledo during the boom days following World War I.

ACKLIN HOUSE AT 576 EAST FRONT (BUILT PROBABLY IN 1920S). This Queen Anne house with most of the characteristics of its style easily noticeable is one of several houses in its block that is said to have been moved to their present locations. According to a former owner, this one is associated with the Donald R. Acklin family and originally sat on the river side of East Front Street. Acklin was a member of the Toledo family that founded Acklin Stamping Company and was socially prominent and a widely known horseman.

WALBRIDGE HOUSE AT 28627 STONECROFT (BUILT C. 1917). Known as Stonecroft, this elaborate mansion, one of the first along this part of the Maumee River, was built by industrialist and glass pioneer William S. Walbridge. The three-story house was designed by Toledo architect Harry W. Wachter, assisted by Thomas Best and Horace Wachter. The landscape architect was Olmstead Brothers of Brookline, Massachusetts, who did several of the East River Road estates. The house is of wood, stucco, and brick and is set among deep ravines and a stream. Entrance is gained across a stone bridge. The structure is asymmetrical with a steep roof, rectangle and octagon half-timbered wall patterns broken by diagonal timbering, and massive stone chimneys. A large patio in the rear overlooks the river. Walbridge, born in Boston, joined the Toledo Glass Company in 1898. He was involved early on with Michael J. Owens and Edmund Drummond Libbey (whose sister he married) when they were laying the foundations for the glass industry in Toledo, and was an executive in glass companies and banks.

DUANE STRANAHAN HOUSE AT 577 EAST FRONT (BUILT C. 1917). This river estate, called Needmore, was originally the farm of Col. George P. Greenhalgh, son-in-law and business partner of William A. Walbridge (see preceding page). It was acquired by Duane Stranahan Sr., son of Champion Spark Plug founder Frank D. Stranahan, in the late 1930s. The architect for the building was Toledo's Mills, Rhines, Bellman & Nordhoff. Landscaping was created by Ellen Shipman, the interior design by Helen Irwin, and the outbuildings by Alfred Hopkins, all of New York. The house is Colonial Revival in style, built of fieldstone and clapboard with the cornice running the full length of the building. Chimneys are on the ends for visual balance. Wings on the right side are clapboard while the main section is stone. Windows are straight-topped and rounded. The outbuildings (former stables and guest houses mainly) are examples of the Federal style. Through efforts of the late Mrs. (Virginia) Stranahan, the entire property is now permanently preserved as a public learning facility called the 577 Foundation. (*below*) The former V-shaped stables housed the show and polo horses of Greenhalgh, an avid horseman and artillery officer in World War I. When Carranor (see page 36) won the Midwest Circuit of the National Polo Association championship in the 1920s, ponies were brought into this open area for accolades and goodies during an outdoor dinner celebration.

SECOR HOUSE AT 109 ROCKLEDGE DRIVE (BUILT C. 1920). This house started as a large summer cottage like a number of others along the "Gold Coast" of East River Road. In 1929, architect George B. Rheinfrank Sr. designed the remodeling of this building into a permanent home for the Jay K. Secor family, and eight years after his death, his widow had it complete in its present form. The large estate that extended across River Road was called Rockledge and was a working farm with several living quarters for employees, along with stables and a barn at the far end of the property. Several of these buildings are now private homes. The property on the river side was earlier owned by another prominent Toledoan of the time, F. B. Shoemaker, who was one of the very first to venture from the comforts of the city this far up on our side of the river. Secor was the son of a well-known Toledo family active in the wholesale grocery and banking business. He was senior member of the brokerage firm of Secor & Bell, later known as Secor, Bell & Beckwith, and was prime promoter and president of the company that built the Secor Hotel in 1908. Fourth generation descendants are still residents in the house, and most of the surrounding acreage has now been developed.

AMERICAN FOURSQUARE HOUSE AT 718 SANDUSKY (BUILT IN 1920S). This brick house, builder unknown, represents a particular simple-plan eclectic style called American Foursquare that falls within a category of architecture known as Prairie, which originated in Chicago. Foursquare is a term relating to a family of shapes that became the main criteria for its labeling—in this case a box-like shape with a low-pitched hipped roof and single-story porch with an off-center entrance, all typical of this subtype.

Notice the variety of brickwork (best appreciated by a walk around it). This includes a vertical belt course at the top and bottom of the first and second floors, horizontal decorations across the front beneath the eaves, and segmental arches over the downstairs side windows.

YARYAN HOUSE AT 534 EAST FRONT (BUILT IN 1920S). Amidst so many Victorian houses on this street, it is a shock to come across this Spanish Eclectic structure built by Homer L. Yaryan. While there are many subtypes of Spanish architecture, this one best reflects the Mission style with its red half-cylinder tile roof, one-story porch, arched entryway, stucco walls, and iron decorations. Yaryan was the owner of a car agency and later was a coal dealer. He was a member of the family involved in providing Toledo users steam heat, a by-product of the generation of electricity at the old downtown Toledo Edison plant.

PALACE THEATER BUILDING AT 218 LOUISIANA (BUILT IN 1921). Charles F. Bayer, a harness, buggy, and farm implement dealer, invested in this building, Perrysburg's first movie house. A 208-seat theater, it offered motion picture and live stage entertainment until 1957. It is said to have been the first and smallest movie house in Wood County to offer "talkies." A 1923 alteration made space for a shop left of the entrance, and there have been other changes. Bayer was born in a log house south of town. He moved into Perrysburg to start his business in 1898 and later operated a coal and feed store.

SUPERIOR STEEL WOOL BUILDING AT SIXTH AND MULBERRY (BUILT IN 1921). About 85 years ago, a local civic group lured the construction of a factory for a relatively new consumer product, steel wool. Enthusiasm was high, based on available new machinery that would greatly increase normal production over that of the half dozen other factories in the country then making the product, and because the operation would be largely locally owned and run. Architect Harold H. Munger designed this then state-of-the-art 100-by-140-foot building that then consisted of the twin two-storied sections and the one-story part in between. Walls were largely of glass to help provide interior lighting. Because the product was relatively unknown, it was thought wise at the outset to set up temporary facilities elsewhere for an exclusive demonstration for ladies to show its various uses for kitchen cleaning purposes. (It was also considered a good gimmick to entice more local sale of stock.) Unfortunately, by 1929, the factory here was in receivership, and the facility was later adapted and enlarged to accommodate Peters Stamping Company, and since then succeeding metal-oriented firms.

MACNICHOL HOUSE AT 30217 EAST RIVER ROAD (BUILT IN 1921). George P. MacNichol Jr., a glass industry executive, built this house on an estate he called Orchard Bend just outside of town. Designed by Mills, Rhines, Bellman & Nordhoff of Toledo and built by the Carl Ruck Construction Company, it makes use of Queen Anne and Tudor details best appreciated by viewing all sides. Half-timbering is visible at the lower left in this picture. The river side has a combination of patterned brick, half-timbering and stucco and an interesting use of windows and dormers. Landscaping was done by A. D. Taylor of Cleveland, and the interior was designed by Hester Mills of New York City. MacNichol, whose grandfather was the Edward Ford who founded what was to become Libbey-Owens-Ford, came here from Wyandotte, Michigan. He grew up in Toledo but moved here when other prominent Old West End families chose East River Road for their permanent homes.

FORD HOUSE AT 29755 SOMERSET ROAD (BUILT IN 1922). By far the largest in the Toledo metropolitan area, if not Northwest Ohio, this mansion off East River Road was built by George R. Ford Sr. The huge building, based on 17th-century English style and now a part of The Hamlet development, was designed by Mills, Rhines, Bellman & Nordhoff of Toledo. Brick trimmed in sandstone, it had as many as 84 rooms, including 11 bathrooms and 13 fireplaces, plus a ballroom. The interior and landscaping was done by New York firms. Originally consisting of 80 acres, Ford sold a portion to his brother-in-law W. W. Knight Sr. They also shared ownership in much adjacent acreage, including the Belmont Farm, which produced fresh produce, milk, poultry, and prize-winning cattle. Outbuildings still in use or converted include a gatehouse, guest houses, garages, a greenhouse, and a gardener's cottage. Alterations include a two-story wing added onto the left side and the division of the entire house into three separately-owned living quarters. Irreplaceable interior ornamentation remains intact. Ford was a third-generation glass manufacturing executive whose grandfather built the first plate glass works in America and whose father founded what became Libbey-Owens-Ford.

TACK ROOM AND GROOM'S COTTAGE. The tack room and groom's cottage were attached to the horse barn shared by the Ford and W. W. Knight families. It is now a residence.

FULLER HOUSE AT 28589 EAST RIVER ROAD (BUILT IN 1923). Rathbun Fuller, the Toledo son of Civil War general John W. Fuller, built this house of a Mediterranean architectural mix. It was designed by Perrysburg architect George B. Rheinfrank Sr. and features mottled tan brick with stone trim and a red tile roof. The front entrance is under a flat-topped loggia supported by Doric columns, above which is a large Palladian window. The estate is called The Terraces. Fuller, once called the dean of Toledo lawyers, was legal counsel and director of several major firms and was a founder of Toledo Trust Company. He was once a U.S. commissioner and deputy clerk of the U.S. District Court.

MATHER HOUSE AT 30027 EAST RIVER ROAD (BUILT C. 1925, NOW RAZED). This huge, virtually irreplaceable mansion was built during a three-year period by Gordon M. Mather, founder of the former Mather Spring Company. He named the estate Belle Alliance. It typified Queen Anne architecture and was designed by Mills, Rhines, Bellman & Nordhoff. The interior was done by Herter Looms, Inc. of New York and the landscaping by A.D. Taylor of Cleveland. Built of brick, timbering, stucco, and marble, the structure featured two wings with a gallery hallway between, a castellated parapet, a sculptured classic doorway with fluted pilasters, and marble trim throughout, especially around the primary entrance. The massing of gables and the five stark chimneys are eye-catching, and a huge and elaborate garden and lawn in the front with a pond and statuary made this a truly spectacular property. Mather was born in Louisiana and came to Toledo in 1911. His company became one of the largest automotive industry suppliers in the nation.

REPLACEMENT. After becoming part of a development, the Mather mansion was torn down in 1985 and replaced by this large version of the original.

BENTLEY HOUSE AT 30465 EAST RIVER ROAD (BUILT IN 1926). Woodgate was the name of the estate and home chosen by Thomas Bentley, owner of the A. L. Bentley & Sons Construction Company. Representing one of many subtypes of Georgian architecture, this three-story house with a slate hipped roof and one ell angling slightly has dormers, windows horizontally and vertically aligned, decorative keystones above each window, and the cornice emphasized by tooth-like dentils. The two-car-wide porte-cochere with balustrade replaced a narrower original one, and the eight-foot-tall windows on the downstairs right were originally double-hung and had shutters. It is interesting that the only wood used in the framing of this house was for the roof rafters. The floors, walls, and partitions are reinforced concrete and masonry. Bentley was the son of Anderton Bentley, who came here from England to found the firm in about 1872. The firm built many of the Toledo area's major buildings and other structures throughout the country.

CITIZENS BANK BUILDING AT 114 LOUISIANA (BUILT 1926). Designed as an Italian Renaissance-style building by Simons, Brittain and English, Inc. of Pittsburgh and Columbus, this structure housed the former Citizens Banking Company and has an Indiana limestone facade with a parapet at the roof. A massive stone arch dominates the front, at the top center of which is a scroll-shaped bracket decorated with acanthus leaves. Within the arch is a large window, and at the street level are two narrow windows with wrought iron grills. On the left side of the building are three Romanesque arches with scroll-shaped keystone brackets.

BOWERS HOSPITAL AT SECOND AND LOCUST (BUILT LATE 1800S, RAZED IN 1965). Now a vacant lot, this modest building sat on this spot as a small private hospital first owned and operated by Canadian-born Dr. Isaac S. Bowers. When it was built is unknown, but it was known as the Tyler residence in about 1911. Quite possibly the wing on the left was an addition. Over its 40-year existence under different ownership, it became Community Hospital, then later Perrysburg Hospital. Isaac Bowers served as mayor.

Mrs. Edward Ford House at 28523 East River Road (Built in 1927). Sitting far back from a formal entrance is the manor house of an estate called Graystone built for Mrs. Edward Ford. The house is of Tudor or Jacobethan Revival style and was designed by Toledo architects Mills, Rhines, Bellman & Nordhoff. The style was popular in this country from the late 1800s through the 1930s. It emphasizes gabled roofs, elaborate chimneys, and the familiar half-timbering, which mimics Medieval in-filled timber framing. The Tudor entrance is set within a gabled projection with a bowed bay window, and on the right side at ground level are narrow stone-mullioned leaded glass windows. Like others along this part of the road, the rear of this house offers an excellent view of the river. Carrie Ross Ford (for whom the city of Rossford was named) was the widow of the founder of what became Libbey-Owens-Ford (now Pilkington Glass Company). She was a Zanesville, Ohio, native.

STRANAHAN HOUSE AT 30209 MORNINGSIDE DRIVE (BUILT C. 1927). Just off East River Road is this castle-like mansion built by Champion Spark Plug's Frank D. Stranahan. Called Wamstan, the place evokes the grand manner of France, England, and Germany, and was designed by architect Charles Schneider of Cleveland. Olmstead Brothers did the landscaping. The building is eclectic, combining Norman Chateauesque, Swiss Chalet, and Queen Anne features, and it required skilled craftsmen to be brought here. The three-story structure has cream-colored stone walls, round turrets, steep gables, varying large corbeled brick chimneys with capstones, and large expanses of half-timbered walls—all in all, a picturesque sight. Up until recent years, it stood alone at the edge of an expansive manicured front lawn, with a large gatehouse and multi-car garage and one-time stables and greenhouse on the property. Stranahan and his brother Robert and their mother founded Champion in Boston in 1910 and almost immediately moved it to Toledo. Frank Stranahan lived in the house until his death in 1965.

STRANAHAN GATEHOUSE AT 30003 MORNINGSIDE DRIVE (BUILT C. 1927). Its exterior virtually unchanged from when it was built, this attractive home began as the gatehouse and 8-car garage for the 12-acre estate of Champion Spark Plug founder Frank D. Stranahan. It was designed by Cleveland architect Charles Schneider and contains a combination of Norman Chateauesque, Swiss Chalet, and Queen Anne features. The building is of solid masonry with foot-thick walls and iron-beam framing. The estate manager lived on the second floor, and the first consisted of eight garage bays, a grease pit, a small office, and a toilet. The left wing of the L-shaped building features an entrance under an intricately carved wooden portico. Half-timbering and stucco decorate three of the gables, and the large original cobblestone courtyard in the back is dominated by a huge surviving American elm tree.

LEWIS HOUSE AT 28503 EAST RIVER ROAD (BUILT IN C. 1928). A single photograph does not do justice to this handsome limestone French Renaissance Revival house that sits far back at the end of a row of carefully trimmed and shaped French Linden trees. It was built by Frank S. Lewis and designed by architect George L. Walling—though the interior design director of *Elle Design Magazine* confirms that it is a copy of a famous 18th century hunting lodge still standing near Versailles, France. Its name is the Pavillon de La Lanterne, but the Lewises called their estate Chanticleer. The front entrance has a slightly projecting extension capped with a carved stone segmental pediment. L-shaped, the building's service and garage wing on the right has a dormered mansard roof. Lewis joined his father and a brother in a Toledo law firm after graduating from Harvard, and it later became the partnership of Doyle and Lewis. He became a noted corporation attorney and civic and social leader, sharing the latter with his wife, Ethel Chesbrough, who was a member of one of Toledo's oldest and most prominent families. (*right*) The gateposts of this estate are topped with proud bronze roosters.

SCHALLER MEMORIAL AT 130 WEST INDIANA (BUILT C. 1928). In 1921, Frederick Schaller, a retired farmer, walked into the office of a Perrysburg man and dumped on his desk a sack of gold pieces, stacks of currency, and a packet of Liberty Bonds (all totaling $6,000) and said he was giving it to the American Legion post for a community memorial to his two children who had died in infancy and to local war veterans. It took nine years before this Neo-Colonial Revival building was erected, just beating the deadline Schaller had set, after which the money was to be returned to his family. It had required two public fund raising drives for another $16,000 to meet the inflated cost. The city donated the land for it. It was designed by local architect Harold H. Munger of Britsch & Munger and is one of several buildings outside the Historic District that is on the National Register.

FREDERIC SCHALLER. Schaller farmed about three miles west of town along River Road. Born in Switzerland, he came here in 1851 and was a Civil War combat veteran.

KUEHN HOUSE AT 572 EAST FRONT (BUILT IN 1928). Perrysburg architect Harold H. Munger designed this Tudor-style house for the Ernest Kuehn family. It features several steep side gables, at least two with the tops clipped or receding, a central tower with parapets or battlements, and an arched stone-edged doorway under a matching window and wrought iron grille. Inside is an enormous sunken living room. Kuehn was associated with an ice cream company, a Toledo dry goods firm, and an oil company.

SPECK HOUSE AT 731 HICKORY (BUILT IN 1932). Claire H. Speck, a Toledo banker who grew up in Pemberville, bought two acres of what was an orchard at the edge of town for his house. Perrysburg architect George B. Rheinfrank Sr. designed the building, called a Georgian-style farmhouse with its box-like shape, side-gabled roof, and symmetrically placed multi-pane windows. Part of the frame of a small existing house on the property was used for the living room of the new house, and hand-hewn beams from an old barn were placed in the ceiling. Wide plank pine flooring also came from the earlier building there. Speck began in banking in Pemberville and Perrysburg, then headed an institution that became State Bank of Toledo and finally Huntington Bank.

INDEX

In the following index of buildings and places described in this book, the street number of each is given in numerical order. In those cases where a street number is not available, the intersecting street indicates the corner where the structure or place is or was located.

STREET NO.	STRUCTURE	
Fremont Pike		
10302	Simmons House	82
Fifth Street West		
138	Smith House	45
202	James Hood House	48
Five Point Road		
	Hazel Farm House	46
Front Street East		
125	John Hollister House	12
125	Halsted House	25
128	Ross House	64
208	Lock House	62
215	St. Rose Church	89
220	Lock Family House	81
228	Rheinfrank House	91
239	Ladd House, 66	
241	F. R. Miller House	67
248	Danz House	96
308	Cook-Finkbeiner House	62
315	J. M. Hall House	41
321	Hunt House	53
332	Strain House	57
333	Henry E. Averill House	70
345	Henry P. Averill House	29
402	Norton House	46
409	Cook House	69
417	Slevin House	58
420	Veitch House	101
424	Harry Barton House	86
534	Yaryan House	112
535	Old Courthouse	56
566	Bates House	45
572	Kuehn House	125
576	Acklin House	107
577	Duane Stranahan House	109
577	Woolfert Cabin	10
Front Street West		
At Louisiana	First Courthouse	10
At Louisiana	Hood Park	98
At Louisiana	Hood Park Monument	98
115	Getz House	54
115	Rheinfrank Hospital	54
140	Exchange Hotel	14
146	Pierce House	79
220	Jones House	51
224	Webb House	30
232	Sargent House	90
304	Powell-Denison House	72
308	Hamilton House	63
320	Van Soyse House	63
326	Stubbs House	43
340	Douglas House	71
341	Former Convalescent Home	95
345	Dodge House	83
348	Lindsay House	17
401	Comstock House	92
407	B. F. Hollister House	21
420	Houston House	44
426	Thornton House	65
502	Crook House	52
503	Spink House	13
508	Maddy House	90
510	Perrin House	32
514	Spafford House	27
538	Powell House	11
Hickory Street		
529	Way House	19
731	Speck House	125
Indiana Avenue East		
208	Fink House	55
Indiana Avenue West		
130	Schaller Memorial	124
220	Frank Thornton House	104
240	Old County Jail	35
343	Yeager House	20
Locust		
76	Roby House	21
80	Bingham-Foley House	22

Louisiana Avenue

102–104	Centennial Block	76
103–105	Old Masonic Building	66
106	Hollenbeck Building	99
110	Old Exchange Bank Building	65
111	Moser Building	96
112	Syndicate Building	97
113–115	C. A. Hoffman Restaurant	47
114	Citizens Bank Building	119
116	Witzler Building	31
117	Ammon Building	78
128–130	Phoenix Block	16
131	Perrysburg Banking Co.	100
200	Houston Building	58
201	Eberly Building	59
203	Fralic Building	101
209	Schlect Building	94
218	Palace Theater	112
219	Lucas Building	75

At Indiana

	Old School Buildings	37, 38
976	Wieland House	73

Morningside Drive

30003	Stranahan Gatehouse	122
30209	Stranahan House	121

Mulberry Street

329	Second Zoar Church Building	60

At Sixth

	Superior Steel Wool Building	113

River Road East

28503	Lewis House	123
28523	Mrs. Edward Ford House	120
28589	Fuller House	116
30027	Mather House	117
30217	MacNichol House	114
30465	Bentley House	118

River Road West

27340	Aurora Spafford House	13

Rockledge Drive

109	Secor House	110

Sandusky Street

718	American Foursquare House	111
904	Seiling House	80

Second Street East

111	Tyler-Roether Building	73
112	Peck House	50
140	Heckler House	50
200	Presbyterian Church	87
203	Hanson House	75
209	Hoover House	84
214	Hannah House	52
215	Munger House	84
216	Eberly House	40
220	Wm. Barton House	51
221	Hoffman House	86
233	Bloomfield House	26
302	Champney House	57
321	J. A. Hall House	42
331	Old Evangelical Church	33
347	Amos Spafford II House	16

At Locust

	Former Bowers Hospital	119
415	Second Ladd House	107
422	Josiah Miller House	40
425	Stone House	22
502	Carranor Club	36
502	Carranor Depot	36

Second Street West

111–113	Old Municipal Building	105
116	Shepler House	26
145	Spilker House	104
215	Himmelman House	55
223–225	A. M. Thompson House	17
227	McKnight House	59
232	Second Beach House	24
246	Parks House	34
300	Second Powell House	11
305	Finkbeiner House	95
310	Cranker House	18
323	Fitzgerald House	71
342	Beach House	24
377	John Hood House	43
523	LaFarree House	74

Somerset Road

29755	Ford House	115

South Boundary East

At Elm

	Neiderhouse House	102

Stonecroft Drive

28627	Walbridge House	108

Sussex Road

29953	H. L. Thompson House	106

Walnut Street

At Indiana

	Former Second Courthouse	28

At Indiana

	Former Town Hall	68
420	Tolman House	83

Visit us at
arcadiapublishing.com

CPSIA information can be obtained
at www.ICGtesting.com
Printed in the USA
LVHW051712030521
686345LV00011BA/357